*This book is dedicated to
everyone who wants to ignite the flow.*

# THE ZIG ZAG PRINCIPLE

## THE GOAL-SETTING STRATEGY THAT WILL REVOLUTIONIZE YOUR BUSINESS AND YOUR LIFE

### RICH CHRISTIANSEN

SECOND EDITION

# CONTENTS


INTRODUCTION
**DELIBERATE DETOURS: NAVIGATING THE ENTREPRENEURIAL DRAGON'S LAIR** ....................11

CHAPTER 1
**ASSESSING RESOURCES: WHAT'S IN YOUR POCKET?** ...........18

CHAPTER 2
**BEACONS IN THE FOG AND CATALYZING STATEMENTS** .........37

CHAPTER 3
**VALUES—A FIRM FOUNDATION** .......................54

CHAPTER 4
**ZIG NUMBER 1—DRIVE TO PROFITABILITY** ..................... 81

CHAPTER 5
**ZAG NUMBER 2—ADDING PROCESSES AND RESOURCES** .. 108

CHAPTER 6
**ZIG NUMBER 3—ADDING SCALE** .......................133

CHAPTER 7
**GUARDRAILS** ...................... 141

CHAPTER 8
**REWARDS—PLANTING HIDDEN TREASURES** .........................152

CHAPTER 9
**AVOIDING THE ALL OR NOTHING TRAP** ..................... 169

CHAPTER 10
**CONCLUSION** .......................183

# ACKNOWLEDGMENTS

I grew up in a family of four boys. I have five sons. There have only been two women in my life, both angels. My beautiful wife is not only my inspiration, but she is my source of strength and resolve. She was vital in all ways in my writing this book, including the composition of much of the text. My mother died when she was still young, but the lessons that she taught me still burn strong.

I extend my highest respect to my children. They have lived and are living these principles, following my meandering path and improving upon it. At this stage of life, seeing them model these principles for my grandchildren and provide proven guidance to the next generation is the real squeeze in life.

Thank you to Jill L. Ferguson, who is doing the editing, and has been my collaborator in this journey, and to Rick Schank for doing the book layout. Your efforts have brought this book to life in ways I couldn't have achieved alone.

I want to pay special tribute to Curtis Blair for being the guinea pig in the first version of *The Zig Zag Principle*. His contributions and willingness to experiment showed real spunk. We grew that little lab rat experiment to $15MM in annual sales and sold it in 2019.

I also want to give special thanks to those entrepreneurs who have courageously followed the principles and proven these models to hold water. When all is said and done, more is usually said than done, and I acknowledge your struggle to create and make a marked impact. I find great joy every time I hear one of your stories.

INTRODUCTION

# DELIBERATE DETOURS: NAVIGATING THE ENTREPRENEURIAL DRAGON'S LAIR

It has been twelve years since I originally launched *The Zig Zag Principle*. Oh, what an amazing ride it has been! In recent years, I've had countless requests for two things: first, an audiobook, and second, an updated revision. I am so proud of the impact that Zig

Zag has had over the years. It has helped tens of thousands of lean startup entrepreneurs launch with success. This was the best I had at that stage in my life.

Now, as an older, more battle-wise entrepreneur, there are a few places in the book that make me cringe. I think, *Oh, there was a better way to do that,* or, *Ah, I should have shown this more efficient tool.* What strikes me the most is that at that stage of life, I was still trying to prove I was the man. I must apologize to my readers if, at times, I came across as operating from a more egocentric place.

In this revision, I have done three major things. First, I've tightened up the narrative and stories to make them relevant to the present day. Second, I've provided my upgraded tools and processes to help you be more efficient in your zigzagging. Third, I've made this book about you and your success, providing relevance and simplicity in areas that were confusing or conflicted in the previous version.

Another key thing I did in this revision was to provide some of my most recent tools on how to operate more consistently in flow, live in balance, and find the middle way. Entrepreneurs are some of the most dysfunctional functional people on this earth. As a wiser, older entrepreneur, I now understand that burning ambition and public success do not bring happiness. In my latest two bodies of work, Legado Family and *BlindSighted,* I cover important aspects of family and community stability, along with finding yourself and learning to love yourself. At first glance, these concepts might not seem to align with entrepreneurship, but I've learned that they are the rocket fuel for becoming a true impact entrepreneur. I have included some of this content where appropriate.

This is where *The Zig Zag Principle* began for me. When my

son was fourteen, I took him skiing for only his third time. Getting off the lift, we accidentally took a wrong turn and ended up with nowhere to go but down a ridiculously steep black diamond run. As we stood at the top of this cliff, my inexperienced skier son looked down in sheer horror and exclaimed, "I am going to die!"

In an attempt to calm his understandable fears, I explained that he didn't need to head straight down the mountainside. Even an expert skier would survey the drop we stood at the top of and decide to zigzag down the steep slope. I instructed him not to look at the bottom of the run but to focus on skiing to a point across the hill and, once there, to turn and ski back across the slope to another pre-selected point.

As a concerned father, I knew my son's chances of getting to the bottom without breaking his leg or neck were far greater with this approach than if he had just barreled straight down the mountain. No question, it took us a while to make our way down. But as he stood at the bottom of the run and looked back up to where he had started, he realized the full import of what he had accomplished—and the lesson he had learned.

Fast forward to today, and I find myself teaching my grandchildren the same lessons. Our fast-paced world has embraced innovative learning modes, from online courses to virtual classrooms and interactive simulations. Just as my son learned to navigate the ski slope, today's students are learning to navigate their educational journeys through a series of strategic steps.

The traditional straight-line approach to education, where one follows a predefined path from start to finish, is being replaced by more dynamic and adaptable learning experiences. These new methods emphasize the importance of flexibility, resilience, and the ability to pivot when necessary. They highlight the value of experiential learning, where students engage in real-world projects, collaborate with peers, and apply their knowledge in practical settings.

As an example, consider the rise of project-based learning (PBL). PBL allows students to work on complex, real-world problems over extended periods. It encourages them to take detours, explore different solutions, and learn from their mistakes. This approach mirrors the zigzag method, where the journey is just as important as the destination. Students develop critical thinking skills, creativity, and perseverance—all essential qualities for success in today's ever-changing world.

Another more dynamic way of learning is through personalized learning platforms that are revolutionizing education by tailoring instruction to individual student needs. These platforms use data and analytics to identify each student's strengths and areas for improvement, allowing for customized learning paths. Just as my son had to navigate the ski slope at his own pace, students can now progress through their educational journeys at a speed that suits them, taking detours to reinforce concepts or explore new interests.

Reflecting on these evolving educational paradigms, I see the value in these new learning approaches. They prepare us not only to reach our goals but to enjoy and learn from the journey. As I teach my grandchildren these lessons, I emphasize the importance of being adaptable, patient, and open to new opportunities. Life, much like skiing down a mountain or navigating an educational path, requires us to take deliberate detours to achieve meaningful success.

When I was younger, I thrived on starting, growing, and selling businesses—fifty-one of them to be exact. But over the past four years, much of my work has focused on helping people operate more in flow and get out of force cycles. I've accumulated a fair share of battle wounds, but I've also gained invaluable tools and models that can help navigate these detours more effectively. My experiences have given me deeper perspectives on operating in flow and understanding what true success looks like. It's not just about reaching the destination but about the quality of the journey and the growth that happens along the way. I have learned to connect deeply with all aspects of myself and embrace the complexities that come with true self-awareness.

## COMPONENTS OF THE ZIG ZAG PRINCIPLE

Before you can begin to zig and zag, there are certain foundational elements that you must build upon in order to succeed, as well as some critical tools you will need. This book is organized around the following tried-and-true principles that will help you make your way to the top of any peak you decide to summit.

➤ Assessing Resources

➤ Identifying Your Beacon in the Fog

➤ Creating Catalyzing Statements

➤ Driving to Profitability

➤ Defining Processes and Adding Resources

➤ Scaling Your Business

➤ Staying within Your Guardrails

➤ Developing Reward Systems

➤ Avoiding the All-or-Nothing Trap: Finding Balance and Joy (with a focus on operating in flow)

Chapters 1-3 provide your foundation, which I like to compare to a road trip. Think of the resources as your vehicle. It may be an old clunker that, on a good day, may get you across town. It may be a jacked-up, high-powered four-wheel drive that knows no fear. Or it may be a vintage Mercedes convertible that you'll only drive when there is not a cloud on the horizon. Think of the Beacon in the Fog as your destination. When you jump in your car in New York City and decide you're heading to San Francisco, there's no way you can see the Golden Gate Bridge. But you know it's there, and, if you're smart, you've mapped out a route that will take you there. Think of Catalyzing Statements as the fuel that will get you to your goal. Once you get the foundation for your business in place, then you can begin to zig and zag. The Zig Zag Principle for growing your business follows a specific pattern:

➤ Zig #1: Always Get to Cash (Chapter 4)

➤ Zig #2: Adding Resources (Chapter 5)

➤ Zig #3: Scaling the Business (Chapter 6)

In Chapter 7, we'll discuss how important it is to establish your own personal guardrails so you don't find yourself driving off a cliff as you fly down the road. I'll share mine and encourage you to find yours.

Chapter 8 introduces the concept of reward systems. Zigzagging is hard work. And now and then you need to pause and reward yourself, your associates, and those family members and friends who are supporting you.

Chapter 9 focuses on avoiding the all-or-nothing trap. Here, we'll delve into how to get into flow and find the balanced, safe, and joyful spot in life. This chapter will be dedicated to helping you understand how to operate in flow and avoid the pitfalls of force cycles, ensuring you achieve sustainable and fulfilling success.

This book is a step-by-step, tactical guide. It is not a theory or a vague concept. You will get practical application tips you can use to succeed, not just in business but also in your life. In addition, you will be provided with a suite of resources and tools that you can use online and offline to assist you in your progression.

In my years in business—whether working for someone or pursuing my own dreams—I have experienced both failures and successes. Many of the failures were due to trying to go straight for the goal and then running out of resources before hitting profitability. Try not to be like me in that regard. *The Zig Zag Principle* is not easy. It requires discipline, hard work, tenacity, and focus. It is not a lazy person's game.

# CHAPTER 1

# ASSESSING RESOURCES: WHAT'S IN YOUR POCKET?

After I wrote my first book, *Bootstrap Business*, which told the story of how my partner, Ron Porter, and I took $5,000 and within one year grew it into a $1.2 million business, I had the opportunity to be interviewed by Garrett Gunderson for a national radio show. Garrett is the author of the *New York Times* bestseller, *Killing Sacred Cows*, and he started the interview by asking, "Rich, tell me about how you started this last business." I said, "Oh, I took $5,000 and…" Garrett interrupted me mid-sentence and said, "No! No, you didn't."

I was kind of stunned and tried to explain, "Well, yes, I actually *did* start it with $5,000." He corrected me again, "No, you didn't." And I retorted, "Yes, I did!"

After what I initially thought was a rather awkward beginning, Garrett went on to explain that the $5,000 my partner and I put up was the smallest part of the equation. In fact, in his words, the money was really meaningless. And in making that point, Garrett was teaching an invaluable lesson.

Most people assume we need to have money to succeed in business and to reach our goals in life. If we want to start a business, the reasoning goes, we first need capital. If we're given a major project at work, we immediately want to know what our budget is. If we want to take our family on a much-needed vacation, the first thing we do is check the balance of our bank account (or, if we really enjoy paying interest, our credit cards). That view develops a straight-line mentality as we undertake whatever we have set our sights on—whether it's a house, a business, a contribution to our team at work, a strong marriage and a stable family…you name it. But if all you think in terms of is how much money you need to achieve your goals, you're missing the fact that success is actually the result of identifying and maximizing a couple of foundational resources that have nothing to do with our traditional view of "capital" and have everything to do with zigzagging toward our intended outcome.

The point Garrett was making was that we succeeded because of what he calls "The Value Equation," which is that Mental Capital (meaning our knowledge, skills, talents, and passions) plus our

Relationship Capital (meaning the quality of our relationships with a broad pool of friends and associates) will equal Financial Capital.

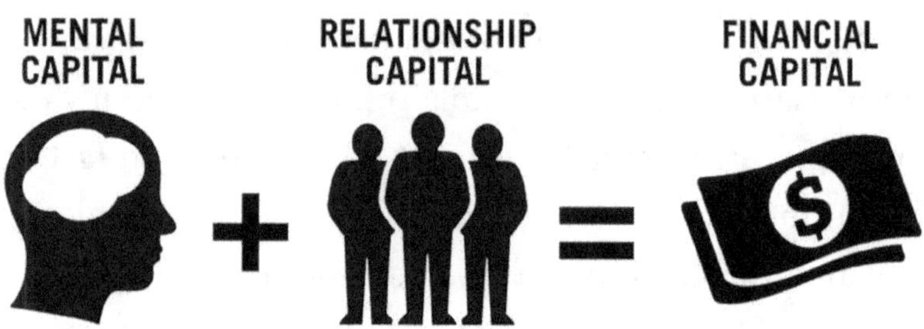



Yes, at some point money is often needed if we are to reach our goals. But that form of capital will grow out of the knowledge and the relationships we have, and the pace at which it grows will be influenced in large measure by our passion. If you need proof of this point, consider this extremely condensed list of transformative businesses that got their start in a college dorm room or garage: Apple, Facebook, Microsoft, Hewlett-Packard, and Google. And while the founders of each of these companies are now household names worth billions, they all began with little more than their smarts and their passion to achieve their goals, combined with their networks of friends.

This view of capital is very different from how most of us think about resources, and most people get the equation backwards. We think, *If only I had some money, I could reach my goals or realize my dreams.* Money cannot build intelligence, relationships, or passion. But intelligence, relationships, and passion can always yield money. Coming to this view, though, may require you to adjust your thinking.

A few years after I graduated from college with a degree in electronic engineering, I enrolled in an executive MBA program while working for Novell, then the pioneer in computer networking (and yet another company founded by four guys with little capital, a bright idea, and a lot of passion—who are now multimillionaires). The vice-president over the division where I worked was an individual named Dave Owens. As I neared the completion of my MBA, I was preparing to move to another division in the company. Before I made the move, Dave called me into his office and asked me a simple question: "Rich, who do you work for?" The answer seemed obvious, and I told him I worked for him. His response was "Wrong!" and that was the end of that meeting.

A week later he called me back in and again asked me, "Rich, who do you work for?" Well, I had been thinking about his question, and this time I confidently told him, "Novell!" Again, he told me I was wrong. A week or so later, his administrative assistant made yet another appointment. I rather timidly went into his office, only to be asked the same question for the third time. But this time when he asked, "Who do you work for?" I answered, "I work for myself."

Finally, I had found the right answer, and as a result my view of resources shifted dramatically. Whether we work for someone or are off on our own, seeing ourselves as the person we work for will light a fire under us to identify the resources we can access, rather than waiting for buckets of money to appear through venture capital coups or budget allocations.

# WHAT ARE YOUR RESOURCES?

Now that you know who you work for, you need to take an honest look at two things: what your resources are right now, and where they can take you.

I currently drive an Audi A6. I love this car, and I love going on road trips in it. One constant over the past 14 years since the first edition is that I still love A6s, and it is still the car I drive. No matter the distance or destination, I know I'm going to get there, and I know I'll travel in comfort. I can sing along with my favorite music on the satellite radio, and my biggest worry is that my speed will creep up to the point where I'll get a ticket. Driving this car is an absolute pleasure!

My Audi A6 is dramatically different from what I drove in college. When my wife and I were first married, we drove a 1972 Dodge Colt that had been wrecked three times. I know people joke about cars that are held together with bailing wire and duct tape, but ours actually was. We tried to improve its appearance by covering up some of the larger dents with a rough coat of Bondo and then painting the entire car with blue spray paint. That plan didn't work very well. In fact, I was so embarrassed by the car that when I was working on my MBA, I would park half a mile away so that no one would see what I drove. The car had a broken oil pan, and the head was cracked. It would get me to school and back, but I never dared take it out on the freeway, let alone on a road trip.

Back then, that was my only resource for getting to my destination. I can go a lot farther now in my Audi A6 than I could in that old Dodge Colt. But the Colt was a lot better than my son's resources when he started a business at age eight. He sold homemade crafts around the neighborhood. When he made his deliveries, his mode of transportation was a kick scooter. So, while my Dodge Colt was constrained by the city limits, his radius was a few blocks from our home. But he made do with the resources at his disposal. His vehicle was different from my A6 and even my Dodge Colt. But it could still take him places.

Of course, the business he was building with his resources was dramatically different than the type of businesses I was able to build. But then, the businesses I build have been dramatically different than the ones Elon Musk has built. I understand he is riding in a rocket ship these days!

Obviously, we can go farther if we have a jet (or a rocket ship) than if we just have a kick scooter. But any one of these vehicles will get us somewhere. We may have farther to go and more zigs and zags to create if we are starting with the kick scooter, but even when we think we have no resources, we actually do. Whatever your circumstances, it is important to look deep down in your pockets.

I grew up in a rural Southern Utah town with a population of about 2,000, if you include the cows and chickens. My family did not have any worldly wealth to speak of. But I had dreams of going to college, succeeding as an engineer and businessman, and moving somewhere a bit bigger than my beloved hometown. When I was a young boy, my resources were the equivalent of my grandson's kick scooter. They consisted mainly of sheer determination, the guts to move forward, time, and boundless energy. I also had a bicycle, which was handy because a nice neighbor who knew I wanted to work offered me a paper route. With that paper route, I was able to save enough money to fix up an old lawn mower that was sitting unused in our shed. After a bit of self-promotion, another neighbor offered me the job of mowing the hospital's lawns. Between the paper route and the lawn mowing, I was able to buy more lawn mowers, and I invited my brothers to help mow other lawns. I kept a percentage of what they earned, which seemed fair because I was supplying the equipment. I saved most of the money I earned and put it toward my goal of going to college. I also worked hard in high school and received a scholarship, which added more resources toward my goal to graduate from college.

It may seem that I traveled in a fairly straight line toward my goal, but if you look more carefully, I did a lot of zigging and zagging. It may also seem that I had very limited resources, but let's review them before arriving at that conclusion:

- ➤ Determination

- ➤ Time

- ➤ Energy

- ➤ Good health

- ➤ Supportive parents

- ➤ A bicycle

- ➤ A neighbor who offered me a paper route

- ➤ An old lawn mower in the shed

➤ Money to fix the lawn mower

➤ Knowledge to fix the lawn mower

➤ Another neighbor who offered me the lawn-mowing job

➤ Friends who wanted to mow lawns

➤ Good grades, which led to a scholarship

I love speaking to young, enthusiastic college students. But whenever I talk about resources, one of them will say, "Rich, it's great you've been able to start all these businesses, but look at where you are!" I then have to tell them that I had to climb the ladder rung by rung, starting at the very bottom.

## MENTAL CAPITAL

I value education. I grew up determined to graduate from college, and I did. Twice. First, I earned a bachelor's degree in electronic engineering (which is not a major I would recommend if you want to sail through college), and second, I earned an MBA.

I give you this background because I don't want you to misunderstand when I say that getting an MBA or any other degree is not mental capital. Information alone is not sufficient. I know enough "educated idiots" who are very book smart but are not able to put what they've learned to good use. Whether your sources of information are traditional or nontraditional, your mental capital is your ability to apply that information. As I wrote in this book's introduction, all the traditional learning models have shifted, and we must adapt, adjust, and change. As Ray Noorda said, "Resist change and die, adapt to change and survive, create change and thrive."

I learned things in my MBA program that have been of direct benefit—lessons having to do with finances, human resources, motivational philosophies, etc. But the greatest benefits came from experiencing the discipline of learning—exploring, digging, experimenting, and applying. I made it a point to continue to explore and discover after I received my diplomas, and I've learned some lessons since that have stayed with me far longer than the content I was tested on in the classroom.

As you assess your mental capital, by all means consider what you've learned in school, but also consider what you're good at. What special skills do you have that you could apply to your current situation? What are you curious about? Do you have unique insight or understanding about a particular field?

For me, I think I have some natural ability as a salesman, which helped me convince my brothers to mow lawns for me. I'm good at understanding technology, something I was aware of when I set out to repair that old lawnmower in my parents' garage. Both are forms of mental capital I've continued to use to this day. Somewhere in my career, I became adept at search-engine optimization, or making sure web sites show up at the top of the list you see when you push "search." That knowledge didn't exist when I graduated from college, but I picked it up along the road and it's paid big dividends.

I have an acquaintance who had a solid career in broadcast journalism when YouTube and digital streaming started to revolutionize the industry. Like many of his colleagues, he faced the daunting task of adapting to the rapid changes brought by digital media. While some resisted the shift, clinging to traditional broadcasting methods, he embraced the new technology. He started a YouTube channel, learned the ins and outs of digital production, and engaged with his audience on social media. His channel grew exponentially, and today he runs one of the most popular and influential news channels on YouTube, reaching millions of viewers worldwide. His success came from his willingness to adapt, learn, and leverage his mental capital in a new and evolving landscape.

Sometimes our schools present learning as a straight line: You learn this, you pass the test on that, you get your diploma, you get your first job, and you move up the ranks. But identifying and applying our mental capital will inevitably lead us to zigs and zags throughout our lives if we are willing to open our eyes to our potential and to the possibilities that lie before us.

Passion is a crucial form of mental capital. It not only fuels our drive but also attracts others to support our goals. In my professional pursuits, I am passionate about technology and about building businesses. Now, technology can be a pretty dry subject, but I can almost guarantee you I'll bring so much passion to any discussion we have that you'll find yourself fascinated before long. Recently, I was given one hour to meet with an internationally known figure to discuss a technology I thought might benefit him. The one hour he agreed to turned into four hours, and at the end of our discussion he introduced me to his colleagues by proclaiming, "This is the *coolest* geek I've ever met!"

Your passions will be different from mine. But find them.

Make sure your own fire is burning brightly, and others will see it and support you in your pursuits.

## RELATIONSHIP CAPITAL

If you take your smarts and your intelligence and do nothing but sit in a dark room and think about how bright you are, then obviously nothing is going to come of them. But if you take your smarts and your intelligence and use them to the benefit of people around you, the relationships you build will propel you toward your goals. Likely, you won't find yourself traveling in a straight line; but, even with twists and turns, you'll get there.

While I was still in college, I worked in technical support for a startup company named Netline. Everyone in the company was busting their guts to make this little leading-edge technology business work, and we had advanced to the point where we had attracted the attention of a billionaire who was coming to see if he wanted to invest in the company.

The day before he was to arrive, we set up a demo wall and prepared everything needed to show him the technology. I was just a peon in this company, but as I was getting ready to leave that night, I noticed our cement floor had not been swept or mopped, and the place was filthy. We were a startup, and we were so focused on the technology that those small details were overlooked. But I guess I had learned enough from my mother to feel embarrassed to have this incredibly successful businessman see our offices looking as they did.

So I drove home and got my wife, and we went back and cleaned the building. As it happened, everyone was gone by the time we started, and the next day I didn't feel any need to point out what we had done.

We made our presentation to the businessman, he was impressed with the technology, and the company got the funding it needed. As we celebrated, there was a buzz about who had cleaned the building; and even though I didn't say anything, someone figured out who had corrected a glaring oversight. As simple as my contribution was, it created relationship capital with the vice-president of marketing, who asked me to be his technician. Before long, he was promoting me within the company and inviting me to travel with him to trade shows.

I didn't have much mental capital at that point, but— without even intending to do so—I formed relationships that have lasted for years, simply by knowing which end of a broom to hold onto.

Several years ago, a young entrepreneur named Emma started a small bakery in her hometown. Emma had a passion for baking and an innate talent for creating delicious pastries. However, she lacked the financial capital to expand her business.

Despite her limited resources, Emma believed in the power of giving and building genuine relationships. She often donated her pastries to local community events, schools, and charities. Her generosity did not go unnoticed, and she became well-known in her community not just for her delicious treats, but for her kindness and willingness to support others.

One day, she decided to take a chance and reached out to a well-known food blogger who had a significant following. Emma sent a heartfelt letter along with a box of her best pastries, not asking for anything in return but simply expressing her admiration for the blogger's work and her desire to share her creations.

The blogger was deeply moved by Emma's sincerity and the quality of her pastries. She decided to visit Emma's bakery and wrote a glowing review about her experience. The blog post went viral, and within days, Emma's bakery saw an influx of new customers. Her sales skyrocketed, and she quickly gained a loyal customer base.

Emma's story didn't end there. The blogger, recognizing Emma's potential and touched by her generosity, introduced her to a network of other influential foodies and local business owners. These introductions opened doors for Emma that she had never imagined possible.

She was invited to collaborate with a local coffee shop, which featured her pastries in their stores. She also got the opportunity to participate in a televised cooking competition, where she showcased her baking skills to a national audience. Each of these opportunities further increased her visibility and customer base.

Emma's success wasn't just due to her baking skills; it was the result of her genuine generosity and the relationships she built through her acts of kindness. By giving selflessly and connecting with the right people, she was able to leverage their influence and networks to grow her business exponentially. Her story is a powerful testament to how giving and supporting others can lead to deep, meaningful relationships and lasting success.

Building networks of relationships does not happen overnight, and it takes attentiveness and hard work. I've seen people who set out with a very clear goal to build a network as quickly as possible. They see their goal, and they see others as a way to reach the goal. And they often bulldoze straight ahead, leaving expendable bodies in their wake. Some of the greatest relationships I've been fortunate to enjoy have come at the end of zigzagging that took place over months and even years—and could never have been envisioned if I had sat down and tried to map out who I needed to know and where knowing them would get me.

As part of my MBA program while I was still working at Novell, I had the opportunity to go on a trip through Asia to study various businesses in Japan, Korea, and China. When I returned, Mitsubishi had just signed a contract with Novell for some strategic engineering work. As it happened, I was the only one in our department who had ever been to Japan. So, even though I did not speak the language, I got assigned to be the strategic engineer for Mitsubishi.

During this time the president of Mitsubishi's PC Division, Dr. Peter Horne, traveled from Japan to Utah several times to meet with Novell's CEO, Ray Noorda. My job was to pick him up at the Salt Lake City airport and drive him to our Provo office, which was about an hour away. I suppose I could have viewed this assignment as something of a chore, but I chose to see it as an opportunity to get to know a very bright, talented, capable individual. So, I would wash my car, (thank goodness, I had recently traded up from the Dodge Colt!) and would try to think of some interesting topics of conversation.

Dr. Horne and I had made the same trip several times when something happened that changed my life. As he climbed into my car on a Wednesday afternoon for another trip back to the airport, Dr. Horne tossed his jacket into the back seat of my car, unbeknownst to me. When we pulled up to the terminal, he grabbed his luggage but inadvertently left his jacket behind. I drove home, dropped off the car for my wife, and then got a ride to a Boy Scout activity I was helping to chaperone.

This was before cell phones, and while I was gone my wife got a frantic call from Dr. Horne letting her know that he had failed to retrieve his jacket and that his passport and wallet were in its pockets. Without a second thought, my wife loaded our three kids (all under the age of six) into the car and drove like crazy up to the airport. My wife and these little kids ran through the airport as fast as they could in order to get the jacket to Dr. Horne before his flight took off. (If you can remember ancient history, this was before the days of airport security.)

A few weeks later my wife received a package in the mail with a beautiful hand-carved jewelry box and a thank-you note. In the note Dr. Horne commented that his wallet had contained a substantial amount of cash and that not one cent had been touched. He expressed amazement that we would have the integrity to return his wallet without even looking inside. He was also grateful that my wife would drive up, even though it was clearly an inconvenience. In a subsequent conversation, Dr. Horne told me that if I ever decided to leave Novell, he would like to talk with me. Indeed, the time did come when I left Novell, and through a series of fortuitous events I became the general manager of Mitsubishi Electric's PC Division in the United States. Meeting Dr. Horne was one of the first real breaks I had during the early years of my career. What started out as a small act of service on my wife's part was rewarded with a strong mentor, boss, and a dear friend. I will be forever grateful to Dr. Peter Horne.

Building relationships is an important and never-ending opportunity that will set the foundation for your zigzagging. It will open more doors for you than you could ever imagine. It's also a process that needs to be looked at from the right perspective. I would recommend that you remember two important principles: First, do the right things for the right reasons. Second, don't ever use people.

We live in a selfish world where some people believe the world stopped revolving around the sun on the day they were born. Some have the mindset that everyone but themselves are disposable and that they can just burn through as many people as necessary to get where they're going. My experience and observations have taught me repeatedly that a far better way to live is to have a genuine concern for others and seek ways to serve those around you. That said, our motivation should never be anything other than doing the right thing.

I recall one young man who I was eager to help. He was incredibly bright and talented, and I saw a lot of potential in him. On several occasions I put myself out there to help him. When I was leaving the department where I had been his boss, I made sure he had a good position. A few weeks later, he complained to me that he was not happy in his new job and was looking for another. I opened my network of friends to him and helped him find new employment. A couple of months later he had burned through those relationships, and I found myself having to apologize to close associates for the messes he had created. I recommended him for several other jobs and offered my advice whenever he called. I even helped him get into a prestigious MBA school.

I never received a thank-you from him, nor any offer to reciprocate for the help I had given him. In fact, one time I asked a very small favor of him, but he was too busy. Another time I overheard him pointing out some of my weaknesses to a group of associates. We should not help others with an eye toward what we can get in return, but when all we get back is a lack of gratitude and a sense of being used, that becomes burdensome. In this case, though my "friend" continued to call for help from time to time, I simply quit responding to his demands and returning his calls. No one likes to feel used.

## APPLICATION

Wherever you are and whatever you plan to do, you'll benefit from making a list of the resources you have at your disposal. Start with what you have today and dig deep down into your pocket. Look for resources that you might otherwise overlook.

## VALUE EQUATION

### Mental Capital + Relationship Capital = Financial Capital

| Value Equation |
| --- |
| List your mental capital: What are you good at? What are you passionate about? What skills do you have? |
| List your relationship capital: Who are ten people that can help you get closer to your goals? |

> If you do not have ten people you can call on, what can you do to build relationships with ten such people? How can you serve these people?

## SUMMARY

In Chapter 1: Assessing Resources: What's in Your Pocket?, the focus is on redefining the essential resources needed for business success. This chapter challenges the traditional notion that financial capital is the primary resource for starting a business. Instead, it emphasizes the importance of mental capital and relationship capital.

➤ **Assessing Resources:** Take an honest look at what your resources are right now and where they can take you. Whether your vehicle is a kick scooter or a rocket ship, recognize and utilize your available resources effectively to reach your goals.

➤ **Mental Capital:** This includes knowledge, skills, talents, and passions. It's not just about what is known, but how that knowledge can be applied effectively. Education and experience are valuable, but the ability to adapt, explore, and apply what has been learned is crucial.

➤ **Relationship Capital:** The quality and breadth of one's network are vital. Building genuine relationships and helping others can open doors and provide support that money alone cannot. Networking should be approached with integrity and a genuine desire to serve others.

➤ **The Value Equation:** Mental Capital + Relationship Capital = Financial Capital. Success often stems from leveraging intellectual and relational assets rather than relying solely on financial resources. Passion and adaptability are crucial in maximizing these assets.

CHAPTER 2

# BEACONS IN THE FOG AND CATALYZING STATEMENTS

Midway through my career, I was working for an incredibly shrewd and successful businessman named Ladd Christensen. One day, in a moment of frustration, he called me into his office and bellowed, "Rich, define 'entrepreneurship!'" I rattled off some lame textbook answer, and he responded, "Wrong. Wrong! Entrepreneurship is having the courage to wander in the fog."

At the time I didn't really buy it. My style was to move from point A to point B in as direct a line as possible. I was (and still am) a goal setter, and wandering aimlessly held no appeal; in fact, it seemed antithetical to getting where I wanted to go, either in business or in life.

Although I disagreed strongly with Ladd at the time, the point of his tirade became much clearer years later when I read an article by a well-known educator and religious leader who told how he had once asked for clarity from his file leader on an assignment and received what initially seemed to be a puzzling response:

> *"The trouble with you is you want to see the end from the beginning." I replied that [yes] I would like to see at least a step or two ahead. Then came the lesson of a lifetime: "You must learn to walk to the edge of the light, and then a few steps into the darkness; then the light will appear and show the way before you."*
> — Boyd K. Packer, "The Edge of the Light," BYU Today, March 1991

Despite my natural inclination to always want to know exactly where I'm headed, I've learned that, whether we're talking about starting a business, completing a complex project our boss has given us, or helping a trying teen get through high school, our lives inevitably involve some wandering in the fog. Very seldom do we have a crystal ball showing us every step we should take and everything that is going to happen.

## FINDING OUR BEACON IN THE FOG

It is one thing to wander aimlessly, which some of us, unfortunately, do. It's a very different matter to identify and set our sights on what I call a big, audacious goal, which becomes our "beacon in the fog." With that beacon firmly in mind, we are far better equipped to head into the darkness, knowing we may not always be able to see where we're going with crystal clarity but still know where we're headed. Airline pilots do this all the time. They barrel through storms and massive cloud banks at 500 miles per hour, unable to see 10 feet in front of them, and we passengers are accepting of this insanity because we know they are fixed on a clearly identified bearing.

If we're smart, we do the same thing. We start out with a big goal to guide us, and every once in a while we hit a smaller goal, which provides a break in the fog that lets us catch sight of our beacon before we take those next steps into the darkness. The process is messier and more risky than it is clean, pristine, planned, and calculated. But if you have a solid, clearly defined beacon in the fog to move toward—and a foundation to travel on—then you will arrive at your destination, just as you've planned. *But only after some inevitable zigzagging!*

In the last chapter, you assessed your resources and figured out what kind of vehicle you have at your disposal to take on your journey to success. Now let's talk about clearly identifying your destination. Where do you want to go? What is your beacon in the fog?

Imagine there are two groups of friends who want to take a trip, and both groups start out with identical resources. The first group spends considerable time researching travel ideas on the Internet. As they explore various options, each mentions a long-held dream of seeing France, so they set a goal to travel there together in one year. When their income tax returns arrive, each person deposits the money in a special fund created just for this trip. They cut expenses wherever they can in order to build their savings accounts. They each get a credit card that gives them double miles, which they then use responsibly (so they're not wasting the money they're saving on interest). They even put their change in a jar at the end of the day.

A year later, they are able to purchase their airline tickets with frequent flyer miles; in fact, they have enough miles to upgrade to those oversized business class seats with the individual video amenities. Soon after, they are ready to take off. They fly into the Charles de Gaulle Airport, then head to the luxurious Hotel de Crillon. While in Paris, they schedule adequate time to stroll through the Louvre and see some of the world's most famous paintings. Of course, the Mona Lisa is at the top of the list. They climb to the top of the Eiffel Tower, counting each step as they go. Their evenings are spent in famous French restaurants that serve *croissant au beurre*, thinly sliced French fries, and sweet crepes. After enjoying Paris, they make their way down the beautiful French Riviera to visit Nice and Cannes. They even take a day trip to Monaco to visit the raceway and winding streets that meander along the sheer cliffs. After spending two weeks of leisurely, deliberate enjoyment, they return home, relaxing in business class.

The other group of friends kind of jump in their car one day and say, "Hey, let's take a trip!" Once they're all in, they open their wallets and see they have a total of $17.93 among them. That doesn't seem like much, but one person has a credit card with a $500 credit line (at 29 percent interest). No one has a strong opinion about where to go, so they flip a coin to see if they should travel east or west. The quarter lands on tails, so they head west. As they leave town, they stop at the local Gas-n-Go to fill up and buy some snacks and soda pop. They charge the credit card for the gas and drinks, and off they go. After about 200 miles, they realize they are in a remote part of Northern Nevada, where the inhabitants consist mostly of rabbits and rattlesnakes. Not surprisingly, they realize they have no idea where the closest town is, which concerns them because their gas tank is getting low and they are almost out of drinks. Suddenly, they begin praying that they have enough snacks and gas to get them back home. And, in the midst of those silent prayers, they find they are getting on each other's nerves.

In both cases, these are trips that are going to be talked about for years to come. But the nature of the reminiscences will vary considerably!

Many people live their lives much like the friends who took the second road trip. They take whatever comes and live day-to-day or paycheck-to-paycheck. They do not have a plan or a goal for where they want to go, let alone end up. There is no beacon guiding them toward where they have determined they want to go.

Finding your beacon is a very personal and individual pursuit, but there are some principles that should guide you. First, you should look for those things you are passionate about and you have the ability to achieve. They should exceed your grasp so that you're pushed, but they should not be so far beyond your reach that they are unattainable.

In *The Seven Habits of Highly Effective People*, Stephen R. Covey talks about our areas of influence and areas of concern. We all have things in our lives where our preferences and choices can and do make a difference. These are our areas of influence. Some are quite simple. For example, what we wear to work, what we eat for breakfast, or even the jobs we choose to apply for are all things that are clearly within our area of influence. Then there are areas that are more complex, but where we certainly do have an influence. If we're part of a management team, we may not have complete control over decisions that are made, but we do have a say. If we're a parent, we can't really force our children to do exactly what we want, but we can certainly influence their behaviors. If we see a compelling social need, we may not be able to solve it single-handedly, but we can make our own unique contribution.

Then there are those things that, no matter what our concerns may be, are not within our area of influence. Because I love being outdoors, I am very concerned about the weather. But, no matter how vocal I may be when I wake up wanting to play golf and find snow on the ground, there is not a darned thing I can do about it. If I work at the lowest staff level of an international conglomerate, I likely will have no real influence on corporate strategies. If I own a small manufacturing business, the price of gas is beyond my control, even though it has a huge impact on my business plan and profits.

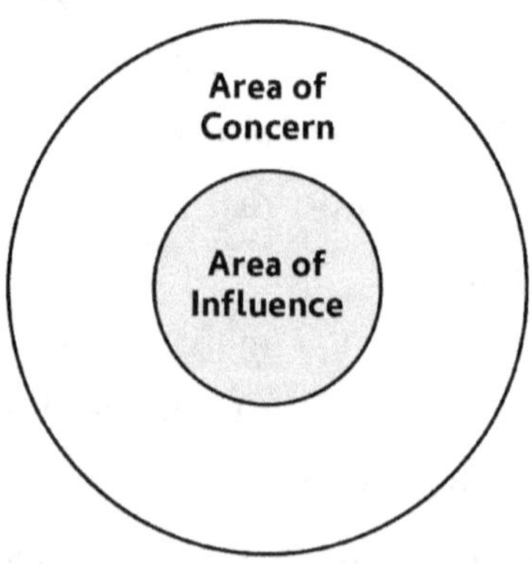

Most people spend 80 percent of their time worrying about things they cannot control. In other words, they spend all of their time and energy focusing on their areas of concern rather than their area of influence. The way to identify those things you want to pursue is to focus right on the border of where your area of influence touches your area of concern. If you establish your beacon in the fog right on the edge of your area of influence, you will find that your area of influence becomes much larger and you will find that your goals, though challenging, actually are achievable.

If we're not setting goals that are within our reach as part of finding our beacon, we will find ourselves doing a lot of aimless wandering in the fog. I've always been motivated by the goals I've set; in fact, every year I see to it that my family gets together and makes goals. These are not your garden-variety New Year's resolutions; these are actual goals we plan to achieve, individually and collectively. We make short-term goals, mid-term goals, and long-term goals. (Personally, I have already set goals through the end of my life.) It has been fun to see the kinds of goals our children come up with each year.

We do not judge each other's goals. We just write them down and post them on the refrigerator. As the year progresses and each goal is met, the children ceremoniously cross off each goal, which brings a huge sense of satisfaction. Sometimes we will put up goals that are a big stretch to reach. Other goals might be much simpler. Over the years my family has found that the best way to make goals is to keep three things in mind. A goal needs to be: (1) written down, (2) measurable, and (3) realistic. It never ceases to amaze me how powerful this simple process of creating and writing down goals ends up being. Of course, times change, priorities shift, and we all do our fair share of zigzagging toward our goals. So, while there are a few goals that end up not being completed, most of what we've committed to gets crossed off by the end of the year. What I find more gratifying than just checking off goals is seeing how my children's goals provide them with direction and motivation throughout the year.

I'll admit there have been times when a family member's goals have left me wondering how they are ever going to achieve them. But I've also seen many examples of how having that beacon in the fog provides a powerful reminder and sense of purpose. My fourth son is our yellow child and always had the family laughing. When he was twelve years old, he wrote down a goal that really made me chuckle. When we asked him what goals he wanted to pursue, without hesitation he blurted out, "I want to go chicken chasing!" We all laughed; but, in keeping with family policy, we wrote it down and posted it on the fridge.

Now, neither do we live anywhere near a farm nor do we have any chickens nearby, so my wife and I were not sure how this goal was going to be met. I suppose we could have driven him to a petting zoo, but in reality, his achieving this goal was not a big priority for my wife or me. When we did think about it, we just figured this would be a goal that would sit on the list and at the end of the year we would say, "Well, sorry, but that one just didn't happen."

The year progressed, and of course there was no chicken chasing. In fact, we thought he had forgotten all about his goal. Then one day in mid-October, my wife called me on the phone, laughing uncontrollably. She and our kids had stopped at the post office to pick up some mail. As they got back in the car, the son who wanted to chase chickens got really excited. He and his younger brother then bolted out of the car and started chasing two wild roosters that had been sitting in the bushes at the post office. My wife and the older brothers watched as these two boys chased those birds around for a good five minutes. My son was so excited when he got home that the first thing he did was grab his big red crayon and cross off "Chicken Chasing" from his list of goals.

While you may never have a goal of chasing chickens, my son's experience exemplifies the power of identifying and then writing down those things that are going to serve as our beacons in the fog. While everyone else in our family had pretty much forgotten about his goal, he kept looking toward that beacon—and for the right opportunity to achieve his goal. I have found that if you put a goal out there and write it down, it is amazing what the universe will return to you.

Your beacons in the fog are generally longer-term goals that your short-term and mid-term goals will lead you toward. You can have several beacons you are working toward in different areas of your life. When I began college, I had identified several beacons in the fog I intended to pursue. One was to graduate from college. Another was to meet the woman I would marry. Still another was to find significant ways to render service. I must say that the day I started college, I had no idea how I was going to accomplish those goals, but those beacons provided me with guidance and motivation as I developed the short-term and mid-term goals that kept me moving toward the light.

After graduating from college (and accomplishing my other two goals), I came up with a new set of beacons that centered around building a strong family, finding success in my career, continuing my education, and finding additional ways to serve. As I found myself approaching fifty, I wanted to find an additional beacon that would motivate and guide me in ways that transcend the businesses.

Finding that beacon took quite some time, but as I searched for it, I realized I have always been concerned about the plight of the poverty-stricken women and children around the world. It just dismays me to see starving children and the abuses of women in developing countries. I have travelled in some of these countries, and I watch the news and worry about these people so much that I developed a rather general goal of helping women in developing countries find their way out of poverty. However, I felt for a long time that this was a goal that was largely out of my area of influence.

Many experiences have helped me change my view, but perhaps none more powerfully than the story of Malala Yousafzai. Malala's journey from being a young girl advocating for education in Pakistan to becoming a global symbol of the fight for girls' education is nothing short of extraordinary. She had a simple yet powerful dream: to see every girl in her community—and eventually the world—receive the education they deserved.

Malala faced incredible adversity, including an assassination attempt by the Taliban when she was just fifteen years old. But her vision remained unwavering. She continued to advocate for education, even from her hospital bed, and her bravery captured the world's attention. Malala's determination and courage expanded her influence far beyond her village in Pakistan. She became the youngest-ever Nobel Prize laureate and has since continued her mission to ensure that all girls have access to twelve years of free, safe, quality education.

Malala's story is a profound example of how setting a big, audacious goal can not only guide us but also inspire and mobilize others. Her vision of education for all girls became a global movement, demonstrating that when we identify and pursue our beacons in the fog, we can achieve remarkable things, even in the face of significant challenges.

## CATALYZING STATEMENTS

Soon after John F. Kennedy became president, he began to see the importance of the manned space program that President Dwight D. Eisenhower had envisioned; in fact, in his State of the Union address in January 1961, he made his support of manned space flight clear. Then on April 12, 1961, the Soviet Union sent the first man into space, which seemed to show the world that while the United States had dreams and ambitions, it was lagging behind in achieving its goal.

President Kennedy did not want to fall behind the Soviet Union, which was putting more money and effort toward space than we were at that time. So, on May 25, 1961, he stood before a special joint session of Congress and outlined what could be viewed as his beacon in the fog. He said:

*"I believe we possess all the resources and talents necessary. But the facts of the matter are that we have never made the national decisions or marshaled the national resources required for such leadership [in space travel]. We have never specified long-range goals on an urgent time schedule, or managed our resources and our time so as to ensure their fulfillment."*

It's important to note that President Kennedy did not stop there. Instead, President Kennedy added what my associate Rick Sapio refers to as a catalyzing statement when he said:

> *"I believe that this nation should commit itself to achieving the goal, before this decade is out, of landing a man on the moon and returning him safely to the earth."*
> —Special address to the United States Congress, May 25, 1961

Of course, that goal was fulfilled when on July 20, 1969, less than a decade after President Kennedy made his famous speech, Neil Armstrong did indeed walk on the moon and returned to earth safely.

Catalyzing statements add specificity and are the fuel that motivates us—and those around us—to keep moving toward our beacon in the fog.

At the risk of sounding immodest, I would say that my beacon in the fog of helping people in developing countries is noble, but it is also too broad. This leads to two problems. The first is that, even though I have a goal, it lacks any specificity to guide my actions day to day. The second is that, as I try to garner support from others, my goal seems overwhelming and unattainable.

So, I refined my goal and concluded I wanted to help educate youth from around the world. Even with that, though, it still lacked focus and was too vague for others to grasp. Eventually, I arrived at my catalyzing statement, which is: "I plan on educating one thousand youth from around the world before I turn fifty." That was the point when I became very focused and also found others who were willing to support my dream. Suddenly doors opened and opportunities arose that helped lead us closer to this goal.

On a very different scale, what I did was much the same as when John F. Kennedy declared, "We will get a man on the moon before the end of the decade…and return him home safely." We must clearly identify our beacon in the fog, and then we must follow that up by creating our catalyzing statement.

As I've come to understand and apply the concepts of beacons in the fog and catalyzing statements, I've watched to see if others who have achieved significant success follow the same pattern. One of the most powerful examples comes from the story of Malala Yousafzai.

Another compelling example involves the transformation of a small startup into a major player in the global tech industry. Consider the story of Netflix. In its early days, Netflix was a struggling DVD rental company. The founders, Reed Hastings and Marc Randolph, had a vision to disrupt the traditional video rental market dominated by Blockbuster. Their initial goal was clear but not widely understood: they wanted to leverage the emerging internet to create a subscription-based service that offered unlimited DVD rentals by mail. It was a radical idea at the time, but it became their beacon in the fog.

Despite numerous challenges and financial struggles, Netflix persisted. They continuously innovated, first by introducing a streaming service that allowed instant access to content, and later by producing their own original shows and movies. Hastings' catalyzing statement—"to become the best global entertainment distribution service"—galvanized the team and investors. This clear, ambitious vision helped Netflix navigate through the fog of industry skepticism and technological hurdles. Today, Netflix is a household name, known for its vast library of streaming content and award-winning original productions.

## DISCOVERING YOUR OWN BEACON

We humans were not designed to sit back and be idle. We are wired to push ourselves to do things of great significance. Steve Jobs made this point in a commencement speech he delivered at Stanford University in 2005:

> *"You've got to find what you love. And that is as true for your work as it is for your lovers. Your work is going to fill a large part of your life, and the only way to be truly satisfied is to do what you believe is great work. And the only way to do great work is to love what you do. If you haven't found it yet, keep looking. Don't settle. As with all matters of the heart, you'll know when you find it. And, like any great relationship, it just gets better and better as the years roll on. So, keep looking until you find it. Don't settle."*
> —"'You've got to find what you love,' Jobs says." *Stanford Report,* June 14, 2005

Goals are what will give you direction as you encounter the fog and darkness that is so much a part of life. Catalyzing statements are what will provide you motivation and fuel as you pursue your beacon in the fog.

To help you identify your beacons in the fog and your attendant catalyzing statements, I want you to complete the following model that Garrett Gunderson has developed (and which I use with his permission). As you work through it, you will find those goals that are unique to you and that will motivate you in ways you might have thought impossible.

Going with your first impressions, brainstorm several answers for each question. You will find that you will end up listing the same situations and/or activities for multiple questions.

| Soul Purpose Finder |
| --- |
| I'm happiest when . . . |
| I'm most creative when . . . |
| What does an ideal life look like for me? |
| What activities make me excited to get up in the morning? |
| The things I am most passionate about in life are . . . |
| When do I feel that I am living my purpose? |
| What hobbies/interests do I have that could potentially cross over as income? |

| What do I regularly get complimented on? |
| --- |
| What talents or activities that I enjoy am I currently being paid for? |
| What areas/activities did I excel in during the past, such as in my childhood/ teenage/college years? |

Now review your answers while looking for trends and similarities. Evaluate which talents, passions, activities and/or interests appeared more than once, and then circle those things. You will then take those and enter them on the spokes of your Soul Purpose Wheel. A wheel signifies motion, and that's exactly what you want to do with the components of your Soul Purpose; you want to put them in motion.

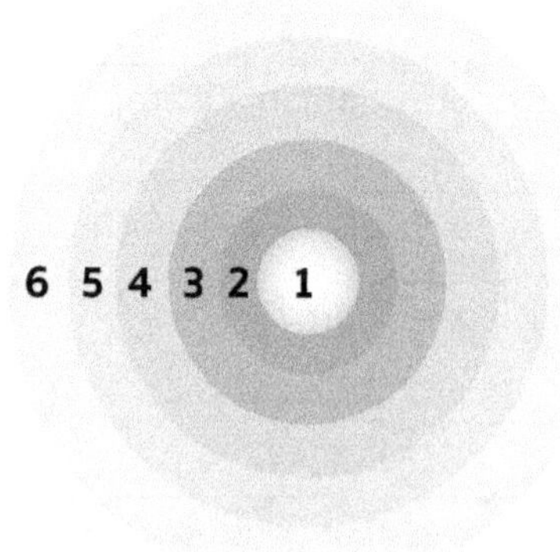


## SUMMARY

In Chapter 2: Beacons in the Fog and Catalyzing Statements, the focus is on defining clear goals and creating motivating statements to guide actions. The chapter highlights the necessity of setting a "beacon in the fog"—a big, audacious goal that serves as a guiding light even when the path isn't clear. It underscores the importance of courage and resilience in navigating the unknown.

➤ **Beacons in the Fog:** These are long-term, clear goals that provide direction and motivation. Having a well-defined beacon helps in making consistent progress even amidst uncertainties.

➤ **Catalyzing Statements:** These are specific, actionable declarations that fuel motivation and help in rallying support from others. They transform broad goals into focused, achievable tasks.

➤ **Goal Setting:** The chapter emphasizes the significance of setting realistic, measurable goals that align with one's passions and areas of influence. Writing down these goals and breaking them into short-term, mid-term, and long-term objectives increases the likelihood of achieving them.

CHAPTER 3

# VALUES—A FIRM FOUNDATION

In the original version of Zig Zag, my focus on values was centered exclusively on business. I've since realized that clarity on your core values is what stabilizes everything you do. As I discuss in one of the final chapters, congruency of values in your personal life, family life, public life, and how we spend our resources enables flow. My experience has shown that of all the concepts in this book and in life, this is how we stabilize. Being clear on your values and having them permeate the organization eliminates brain damage and stabilizes the company. It is the bedrock of culture.

This chapter is one of the sections I have significantly expanded. I consider it the most essential chapter of the book. It might be fun to create businesses around zigging and zagging, but by clearly stating your values and embedding them memorably into your organization, your family, and your life, you eliminate much of the noise and messes instantly.

When we use the word "values," it is often misconstrued. Are we talking about moral values, or what we individually value? The word "values" also feels somewhat antiseptic, and people don't remember overused words like integrity, loyalty, and hard work. Often, when we start talking about values, eyes glaze over and it's blah blah blah.

When the original *Zig Zag Principle* was written, we displayed our values in the form of a mission statement. I have moved away from the term "mission statement" because it was trite, overused, and now comes across as pretentious and sterile. I personally use the word "ethos" because it carries more gravity and feels like part of the air we breathe and the water we drink. However, call it what you will: your operating paradigm, core value statements, or guiding principles.

Values are different from principles. Principles are fundamental truths that cross over all cultures and societies. Values are one level up and require individual determination. Clarifying your core values in business and other areas of your life is the key clarifying factor and the primary lubricant allowing your life to flow.

The way you make your values come to life and breathe vitality and vibrancy into them is by creating stories around them and giving them hang tags—a fun, zippy phrase. Something rooted in passion and a story that the right hemisphere of your brain can grab hold of. Something memorable and vibrant. This is what you publish, talk about, and create stories about. Remember, a culture is created by the stories that are told. You need stories about the rooting of your values. Sure, you want a quick description of the ethos, but what really matters is the energy behind the hang tag.

## VALUES—A FIRM FOUNDATION

Values are the infrastructure or highway system we travel on to reach our goals. If my family and I were taking a road trip to Disneyland from our home in Utah, we would have two choices. We could pull out of our driveway, point our car southwest, and drive through neighbors' dining rooms and yards, cow pastures and weeds, streams, and mountain ranges until we got to sunny Southern California. Or, we could search online for the best route to Disneyland and follow the directions. Option one might get us there eventually if I had an amphibious assault vehicle—and if we could avoid arrest. But I think my family and I would enjoy the trip more if we followed the interstate and exited the freeway once in a while for gas, a bite to eat, and a chance to freshen up.

Just as there are roads my family is willing to take and others we'd rather avoid, there are ways of living life and doing business that I am willing to try and others I steer clear of. For me, I love to drive on paved streets because I know my wife's minivan will get stuck in the mud if I head off across uncharted terrain. And, like a good map, my values keep me on the right roads.

Any organization that is going to be successful—whether it

is a family, a sports team, or a business—must have a set of values to work from; otherwise, it will end up wandering into the weeds.

When I say values, I'm not necessarily referring just to moral values. Values go well beyond what we may typically think of when we hear the word. They are the infrastructure you are going to use as you build toward your goal. Values include the behavior you are going to exhibit, the culture you want to create, and the rules you will follow. Values set the tone for what the culture in the company will be. Following or ignoring values creates the stories that then reinforce the culture we are building. Different families have different values, just as different businesses have different values.

For example, let's suppose you want to start a high-class restaurant with inventive food and a romantic environment. In this restaurant, you would value using fresh ingredients and having a meticulously clean kitchen. Quality, refinement, and culture might be some of the values you would promote among your staff and with your customers (whom you might refer to as patrons). On the other hand, if you were looking to open a family-friendly, fast-food restaurant, you would value speed, efficiency, variety, and the entertainment of kids. Ideally, you would value cleanliness as well. You are not going to use the same high-quality ingredients as your gourmet counterpart, and you might have far more options on the menu, including a kids' menu. Identifying your values, based on your purposes and objectives, is essential so you can clearly define where you're headed with your venture.

Although I do believe in right and wrong, it's important to initially assess your values without judgment. Different businesses must have different cultures and, therefore, values. A collections company that provides a service of calling people and demanding that they pay their bills will value employees who are assertive and who will not back down. The employees would generally value justice more than mercy. They would need to value responsibility and accountability. The employer might value being fair but would define fair in terms of all the parties, with a bias toward the entity that is owed the money.

On the other hand, a company in the business of entertaining people would not flourish if it based its business on the same values as the collections agency. Typically, it would value fun, entertainment, preparation, and social interaction—those values that help ensure that everyone who walks in the door has fun. It would not make sense for the entertainment company to say, "We are an entertainment company that is fair in our judgments." Likewise, you're not going to hear the collections agency say, "We value bringing joy and laughter to our patrons." Different businesses, different values.

I attended a very interesting lecture once where the speaker asked a group of chiropractors the following question: "Are you a healer? Are you a doctor? Or are you a businessperson?" There was a long and awkward pause, and then he continued, "Your response to this question is going to determine how you will set up and conduct your practice." The speaker wasn't suggesting there was a right or a wrong answer; he was saying that the answer would lead each of these chiropractors in a slightly different direction, so they ought to give it careful consideration.

Picture how the "healer" might set up his practice. He would be much more holistic in his approach, focusing on preventative care and wellness. In addition to his services, he might recommend and provide certain supplements and vitamins. He would likely encourage exercise and proper diets. He would certainly teach his patients proper techniques to avoid injury. His values would likely lead him to spend more time with each patient, which he'd need to consider as he mapped out his billing practices. He might spend more time with each customer and may or may not be as profitable.

The chiropractor who sees herself primarily as a doctor is likely more traditional and focuses on getting her patients' spines back into alignment. As such, her need for staff, office space, and billing policies are going to be quite different from the healer. Finally, the "businessperson" would have a dramatically different approach to his practice. He might not even do the day-to-day adjustments, opting instead to have a group of chiropractors work for him. He will be more focused on the production and efficiency of the practice. While these chiropractors' values may differ somewhat, what is clear is that their values are going to provide a road map that guides everything from selecting office space to determining rates to the actual care of the patients.

You can certainly head down the road not really knowing what your values are, but it's never going to get you anywhere good. For many years, my favorite college football team had an incredible coach. He was revered by fans, players, and coaches across the country. He coached the same team for almost three decades and won countless awards, including a national championship. He valued hiring great assistant coaches; and while there was no mistaking who was in charge, he was a delegator.

When he took over his team as head coach, he could see it would never compete well with a running strategy, so he decided he would find quarterbacks who valued passing the ball. He faced teams that could score 20 or 30 points running the ball, but his team could score 40 or 50 by passing. So, they won. Several of his quarterbacks went on to play in the NFL, and more than one took his team to the Super Bowl.

He believed in his coaches, in his players, and in his strategy. On game day, he stood on the sidelines with his arms crossed, completely non-emotional as he calmly kept pace with his team from the sideline. If his team won, his expression was the same as those rare times that they lost.

After this coach retired, a coach came in who didn't seem to know what he valued. His offensive strategy seemed to change from week to week. He would start a quarterback, pull him out, and then try another quarterback. At times, he let his assistant coaches do their jobs, and other times he would take over—sometimes in the middle of a game. When a game was close, he would run up and down the sideline, waving his arms frantically over what was happening. Players and coaches alike didn't know what he expected of them; and, as a fan, it was confusing to watch the team during this time. No one seemed to know what he valued, and, as a result, it wasn't long before he was fired. Since leaving the university, he returned to the ranks of assistant coaches where he has had success, but no one has been willing to offer him a job as the head coach.

The most recent coach of this storied team is almost the exact opposite of the legendary coach. He is much more hands-on, to the point where he has functioned as both head coach and defensive coordinator. He is much more emotional. He is much more involved in the community, and expects his players to be as well. And yet, with all the differences, he is enjoying a winning record that rivals that of the man this school's football stadium is named after. The first coach and the current coach have succeeded with different values systems, but they each have one. And those values were and are crystal clear to each of the players and each member of the staff.

Whether you are deciding for yourself, your family, or your business, the values you settle on will determine your behavior, which will in turn determine what stories will be told about you. These stories will then serve to guide the behavior of those who follow you.

One of my heroes and mentors was a businessman named Ray Noorda. Ray was the CEO of Novell when I worked there, and he guided the company through its "glory days." During his time as CEO, everybody knew very clearly what the values of Novell were. Financial responsibility was at the top of the list. Next was to be on the leading edge of technology. Another was to take good care of customers.

We had a series of mantras that were propagated throughout the company. These were little statements that Ray was famous for, such as, "Resist change and die, adapt to change and survive, create change and thrive." Another was, "Customers first, employees second, shareholders third." One of his statements that used to spread fear throughout the company was, "Spring cleaning whether we need it or not." All of us knew that every spring the bottom 10 percent of performers would be laid off. Ray did not like having dead wood in the company. He felt it was an honor to work at Novell; and if people were not performing, he did not want them to weigh the company down. Not everyone agreed with his values, but these are examples of the culture that Ray created for Novell.

Most of us who worked for Ray considered him to be

something of a tightwad. Whether that is a fair assessment or not, he was definitely fiscally responsible. Although he was a billionaire, Ray did not have a fancy office; in fact, he had the same standard issue desk and chairs as everyone else. When he traveled, he flew coach to save the company money. He did not wear expensive suits. He drove an old 1972 King Cab pickup truck.

Not surprisingly, he loved to walk around the company and meet people. He would stay after hours and talk with the custodians. It was not uncommon for him to come sit on your desk and ask if you had anything good to eat. He would talk to every level of employee. As a result, he knew exactly what was happening in the company.

At one point, we had an executive who made it a point to let others know he had money, and one day he came to work with a shiny new Rolex watch. This employee had failed to take note of the values and culture of the company. Not surprisingly, he was one of those who ended up getting cleaned out the next spring. That became one of the many stories that got passed through the company, which reinforced the values Ray used to guide Novell.

One time I personally witnessed one of Ray's stories, and I did my part to pass it along. I was in the restroom when Ray walked in. There was another man in there who was combing his hair and who kept the water on the entire time he was grooming himself. He would leave the water running while he went to check himself in the mirror. Then he'd come back for a bit more water, and then head to the mirror again. When Ray came in and saw what was going on, he turned the water off. The guy went back and turned it back on—and then gave Ray a dirty look. As the guy turned away from the water, Ray shut it off again. It was obvious this guy had no idea who he was dealing with. After the third time, Ray wagged his finger in this man's face and said, "Waste not, want not." I am not sure what happened to the offender. But I know that I was sure quivering and that the value of not being wasteful was ingrained deep within me that day. These were the stories that would spread like wildfire through the company. They taught the values and created the culture of how everyone in the company was expected to behave.

## VALUES WILL GUIDE US THROUGH THE ROUGH TIMES

I know of a mother who had a lot of children. In fact, some people looked down on her for having so many, but she didn't care. She loved her children. She had very little materially, but she would look at her kids and say, "I will put you up there with the best of them." She had a big goal out there. It was not only to raise good kids: she wanted to raise children who would be hard working and self-reliant. She wanted her kids to go out and make a difference in the world. This was her beacon in the fog.

This family did not have many resources. They lived on a dairy farm at a time when milk prices were dropping. The entire time this family was being raised, there was not one year that their total income was above the poverty level; in fact, many years it was well below the poverty level. But this inconvenience did not deter this mother. She had a set of values she was determined to pass along to her children, and those values guided everything she did. Some of the things she valued were education, hard work, and self-reliance. She did not want her kids to be dependent on society like many other families in their situation.

This mother got creative with the meager resources she had, and she taught her children that if there was something they wanted, they needed to do the same. One of her daughters wanted to take dance lessons like the other girls in her class. This mother talked with the dance teacher; and even though the mother did not have cash to pay for the lessons, the dance teacher happily took milk and eggs from her farm in exchange for those lessons. Another child needed some expensive dental care. The mother went to work at a dental office in exchange for the needed treatment. This family was growing up in the 1970s and '80s before personal computers were common. As her kids became teenagers, the mother would encourage them to take typing classes so they could get a good after-school job. She then allowed the kids to be responsible for their own expenses and learn how to manage their money. As busy as she was and as much as she stressed self-reliance, she always encouraged them in their homework and helped them seek out scholarships.

Once, one of her children was noticing all the name brand clothes her peers were wearing. She stopped the mother and asked, "Mom, are we poor?" The mother thought for a minute or two and replied, "No, we are not poor; we are just broke." She wanted her daughter to realize that even though they did not have a lot of money at the time, they could work hard and move up to become whatever they wanted to be. In her mind a "poor" person was someone with a victim mentality, and she did not want her children to feel as though life was just owed to them.

Another time one of the daughters wanted to try out for the cheerleading squad. Both the mother and the daughter knew the uniforms, shoes, trips, and fees cost a lot of money. So they brainstormed together about how to make this work. The daughter got a summer job moving sprinklers and working at Kentucky Fried Chicken to pay for the things she needed. She had to work a little harder than the other girls on the squad, but those things made her strong.

In the end, every one of this mother's children went to college and then on to productive careers. Each one of these children is contributing to society in his and her chosen field. One is a doctor, another an engineer. There is a nurse, a businessman, a businesswoman, and a teacher. Now that her children are grown, people say to this mom "You are so lucky. How did you do it?" She smiles, knowing it had nothing to do with luck. She had established her goals and values before she even had children. And those children were clearly shown the road map they should follow if they wanted to achieve success.

## VALUES ARE NOT ALWAYS CONVENIENT

In 2023, a significant event in the world of professional wrestling highlighted the importance of integrity and community support. Sammy Guevara, a well-known wrestler in All Elite Wrestling (AEW), was suspended indefinitely following an incident during a match where he continued to perform a move despite his opponent's apparent injury.

This suspension was a setback for Guevara, but he chose to handle it with grace. He did not publicly complain; instead, he took responsibility for his actions and focused on improving himself. Guevara reached out to his fans through social media, expressing his gratitude for their unwavering support and acknowledging his mistakes. He emphasized the importance of learning from adversity and striving to be better.

Despite the challenges, Guevara's fans and teammates stood by him, recognizing his efforts to grow and improve. His return to the ring was met with cheers and a warm reception, demonstrating the community's appreciation for his integrity and perseverance.

Guevara's story underscores the principle that upholding values, even in difficult times, fosters respect and support from those around you. It shows that integrity and accountability are crucial, and that a community will rally around those who strive to do better, even after making mistakes.

This story reflects how maintaining values and demonstrating personal growth can resonate deeply with a supportive community, making it a compelling example of integrity in the face of adversity.

## MAKING OUR VALUES CLEAR

When our children were young, we made a family mission statement. Mission statements are a little antiquated now, but my wife and I wanted to define the values that we wanted to live by in our family. Some of the values we listed were:

- ➤ Our family will support each other in our goals and ambitions.

- ➤ Our home will be an environment of safety, love, and respect.

➤ We will provide unconditional love for each other.

➤ We will teach respect for people, places, and things.

➤ We will embrace the value of hard work and leadership.

➤ We will allow each other to make mistakes and grow from these mistakes, but we will encourage each other to reach for higher levels.

➤ We will have positive friendships.

➤ Our family will work together, play together, and stay together.

➤ We will laugh often and savor the good, while fearlessly fighting the bad.

➤ We will act on life and turn negative situations into positives.

➤ We will value learning and education.

➤ Each family member will strive to make a meaningful contribution to humanity.

Our family is far from perfect, but these are some of the values we set out to teach our children. We have the list posted in our entryway, and each member of our family knows what is expected of them. And I'm always amused at the stories our children tell each other and their friends of the funny things that happen in our family as we reinforce these values.

And guess what? It works. Our children, now all grown, attribute these values as one of the primary catalysts for their stability. This really works—I mean, it really works. It works in business, in relationships, in families, and in philanthropic endeavors. It is fun to reflect on this now and see the stabilizing factor this had in my family's lives and now see my sons enacting this in the lives of my grandchildren.

## VALUE-BASED DECISION MAKING

Rick Sapio taught me the basics of "value-based decision making" some 15 years ago. He also refers to "The Doorman Principle," which is defined as "the deliberate practice of defining a set of values and/or rules to dictate who, or what, is allowed to enter into your life or business." In our lives and in our businesses, we must have a "value gatekeeper." In our home, my wife is the value gatekeeper. When she sees one of my sons being rude to his friends, she will call him on it because "We teach respect for people, places, and things." She insists that our kids do their homework because "We value education." She does not let riffraff into our home and encourages our children to have positive friendships.

My executive administrator is the "value gatekeeper" at my office. She keeps the distractions and business snakes out of my life. She is responsible for the final interview of every potential hire. She deliberately does an exhaustive interview to ensure the person is in alignment with the 11 ethos statements of our organization.

If the candidate does not pass this check, they do not get hired no matter how talented they are.

## VALUES EXERCISE

Implementing this exercise will help clarify your core values.

1.  Write down the names of three people in your life whom you most admire or respect and want to emulate.

2.  From the values listed below, circle seven or eight values that best describe each of those people.

3.  The values that appear repeatedly are the ones you value and want to emulate in your life.

## List of Potential Values

| | | | |
|---|---|---|---|
| Acceptance | Attentiveness | Big-thinking | Cleanliness |
| Accomplishment | Authenticity | Bliss | Clear-headedness |
| Accountability | Awe | Boldness | Cleverness |
| Accuracy | Balance | Bravery | Comfort |
| Achievement | Beauty | Brilliance | Commitment |
| Adaptability | Being admirable | Calmness | Common sense |
| Adventurousness | Being dynamic | Candor | Communication |
| Agreeableness | Being earnest | Capability | Community |
| Alertness | Being famous | Carefulness | Compassion |
| Altruism | Being folksy | Caring | Competence |
| Ambition | Being frank | Cautiousness | Complexity |
| Amiability | Being methodical | Certainty | Confidence |
| Amusement | Being personable | Challenge | Connection |
| Amusingness | Being reasonable | Charisma | Conscientiousness |
| Appreciativeness | Being skilled | Charity | Conservativeness |
| Art | Being thoughtful | Charm | Consideration |
| Articulateness | Being | Cheerfulness | Consistency |
| Assertiveness | understanding | Citizenship | Constructiveness |
| Athleticism | Benevolence | Clarity | Contemplation |

Contentment
Contribution
Control
Conviction
Cooperation
Courage
Courteousness
Craftiness
Creativity
Credibility
Curiosity
Daringness
Decency
Decisiveness
Dedication
Deep thought
Democracy
Dependability
Determination
Devotion
Dignity
Diligence
Discipline
Discovery
Diversity
Drive
Dualism
Dutifulness
Easygoingness
Education
Effectiveness
Efficiency
Elegance
Eloquence
Emotional
awareness
Emotional control
Empathy
Empowerment
Endurance
Energy
Enjoyment
Enthusiasm
Equality
Ethics
Excellence
Excitement
Expedience
Experimenting
Exploration
Expressiveness
Extraordinary
experiences
Fairness
Faith
Faithfulness
Family
Farsightedness
Fashion

Feelings
Fidelity
Flair
Flexibility
Focus
Foresight
Forgiving
Forthrightness
Fortitude
Freedom
Freethinking
Friendliness
Friendship
Fun
Fun-loving attitude
Generosity
Gentleness
Genuineness
Giving
Glamorousness
Good-nature
Goodness
Grace
Graciousness
Gratitude
Greatness
Growth
Happiness
Hard work
Harmony
Health
Helpfulness
Heroicness
Honesty
Honor
Hope
Humbleness
Humility
Humor
Idealism
Imagination
Incisiveness
Independence
Individualism
Individuality
Influence
Innovation
Insightfulness
Inspiration
Integrity
Intelligence
Intensity
Intuitiveness
Inventiveness
Joy
Justice
Kindness
Knowledge
Lawfulness

Leadership
Learning
Liberty
Life direction
Life experience
Likability
Logic
Love
Loyalty
Mastery
Maturity
Mellowness
Moderation
Modesty
Motivation
Neatness
Neutrality
Newness
Niceness
Objectivity
Open-mindedness
Openness
Optimism
Order
Organization
Originality
Passion
Patience
Patriotism
Peace
Peacefulness
Performance
Perseverance
Persistence
Playfulness
Pleasure
Poise
Positive attitude
Positivity
Potential
Power
Practicality
Preciseness
Principles
Productivity
Professionalism
Prosperity
Protection
Punctuality
Purpose
Quality
Rationality
Realism
Recognition
Recreation
Reflection
Relaxation
Reliability
Resourcefulness

Respect
Respect for others
Responsibility
Restraint
Results-oriented
Rigor
Risk
Romance
Satisfaction
Security
Self-awareness
Self-improvement
Self-reliance
Self-respect
Self-sufficiency
Selflessness
Sensitivity
Serenity
Service
Simplicity
Smarts
Sociability
Social connection
Sophistication
Speed
Spirituality
Spontaneity
Stability
Status
Steadiness
Strength
Structure
Studiousness
Success
Sweetness
Sympathy
Teamwork
Tenderness
Thoroughness
Tidiness
Timeliness
Tolerance
Tradition
Tranquility
Transformation
Trust
Truth
Unity
Variety
Vivaciousness
Warmth
Wealth
Well-roundedness
Wisdom
Wit

This simple exercise will bring great clarity to what your values are. From my experience, you will end up with about 10 values with which you closely align yourself.

After you have established your values, do not let anyone into your intimate circle who does not fit with your values. Of course, it's naive to think that you will never have to deal with anyone who doesn't share the same values, but I'm talking about your inside circle or trust relationships. That means your important hires, your friends, your partnerships. You need to establish a value gatekeeper that you have complete trust in to make sure that your values are honored. These values help you surround yourself with people who align closely with you.

Each company or organization needs to make its own set of values and rules that it wants to live by. Listing the values that you want to focus on in your organization is not just limited to your business. You should set up values and rules to travel on in other areas of your life where you are striving to reach a goal. Some of these areas could include:

➤ Projects that you are involved in

➤ Charitable groups you are involved with

➤ Organizations that your children are involved in

➤ Your children's friends

➤ Future business decisions

➤ Your personal habits

➤ Your health and well-being

## EXPANSION ON THIS POWERFUL CONCEPT AND HOW I IMPLEMENT AN ETHOS

Here is an important new learning and key update for you. Values are antiseptic, and people don't remember them. It is vital that you identify the value, as this gives context and understanding. However, the second you have the value identified, you need to give it a hang tag—a fun, zippy phrase. This should be something rooted in passion and a story that the right hemisphere of your brain can grab hold of. It must be memorable and vibrant. This is what you publish, talk about, and create stories around. Remember, a culture is created by the stories that are told. You need stories to be told about the rooting of your values.

Sure, you want a quick description of the Ethos, but what really matters is the energy behind the hang tag.

It is a privilege to earn your way into the circle of trust, not a right. My wife and I have often laughed uncontrollably when Robert De Niro in *Meet the Parents* very brazenly kept blocking his new son-in-law-to-be from "the circle of trust." Who figured, De Niro got it right.

Now, how do you keep individuals out who are NOT in alignment with your values or ethos? Rick has a gatekeeper; I have a value screener. Their job is to carefully watch for incongruities through a fun, non-intrusive set of value screening questions. Oftentimes, these are even a bit misleading. They are always unconventional, and you can't fake your way through them. It cuts right to the chase.

One of the most powerful concepts of implementing value screening is that as you encounter conflict or problems in the organization, you can point to the value that everyone has agreed to live by and use this as a buffer. You can use the value as the arbitrator. Oftentimes in life and business, we get bone-on-bone in our relationships because we end up stating, "You did this," or "This happened," or "You are a problem." With values, you can point to the value and say something like, "We are having a value misalignment on _______ and I would like to have a discussion about this core part of our Ethos." This allows you to address the same issue without harsh defensive postures. I love it when my team members approach me with value concerns, and when I mess up, I apologize and state I will do better. Not only are team members held accountable to the Values and Ethos, but so am I. This gives not only me, but my entire team a safe way to approach problems in the organization.

Below is the Value, the Hang Tag, clarifying statement, and the corresponding screening question for each value for my organization.

| Value | Tag Line | Value Statement | Question Screen 1 |
|---|---|---|---|
| Peace / Joy | Flow Not Force | We live our lives by aligning the values in all areas of our life. We also courageously face the grit and grime that stick to us. We don't force things but allow all areas of our life to operate in flow. | You show up at a party or event that you really looked forward to. You are blocked from getting in even though you had an invite. How do you handle it? |

| | | | |
|---|---|---|---|
| Illumination | Clarity in Chaos | We provide resources, tools, and insights that provide a path through the complexities of life. Above all else, we honor our connection to the divine! "I would not give a fig for simplicity, but would give my life to simplicity on the other side of complexity." | What are your practices to stay in tune and focused? |
| Courage | Do the Right Thing Damn the Torpedoes | We stand in our power. We have the courage to do the right thing even in the face of criticism. This sometimes means standing alone, but we courageously stand for good and light and the higher vibrations of life. | If you saw someone aggressively berating someone in public, how would you handle it? |
| Gratitude | Travel - Taste - Touch | We give thanks and acknowledge the amazing gift that this life is. The opportunity to grow and expand our souls, to experience and savor the good and learn from the bad. | What is going wrong in your life right now? |
| Hopeful-ness | Hope Drippers | We believe the best is yet to come. We are positive and are givers, not takers. We expect all that we operate to also be positive and vibrantly looking forward to not dredging through the garbage of the past. | There are 4 donuts and 5 people that want one. What do you do? |
| Authentic Expression | Speak the Truth or Say Nothing At All | We communicate openly and express ourselves freely. We are open to all views and perspectives and welcome new insights and learnings. We do not participate in rigid dogma or suppressive expression. | Tell me about someone in your life who has very different views than you? How do you relate to them? |
| Playfulness | Laugh More Cry Less | This shit is just not that serious. We encourage a balance of intense work, intense play, and intense rest/self-care. | What do you do to cope when really hard things happen to you? What is your outlet? |

| | | | |
|---|---|---|---|
| Optimism | Go For It | We play a big game and expect to have big wins. We live abundantly and energetically repel scarcity. We play to win and do not let small players or naysayers impact our knowing or our potential. | What would you do if you were cooking steaks on the grill and were 2 short to feed your guests? |
| Integrity | Do What We Say | We keep our commitments. Clear communication wins every time. We show up on time, and we are mindful of the energy that we bring to the table. We are givers, not takers, and we bring our own batteries to the party. | Are you a punctual person? Does it bother you when someone is always late? How do you handle it if this happens? |
| Oneness | True Community | We will surround ourselves with a deep connection of trusted community that we can lean on and count on in moments of crisis. We find joy in the deep intimate relationships and exchanges of our souls. | When was the last intimate soul exchange? With whom? How did it happen? |
| Faith | Faith over Fear | We extract the destructive emotions of guilt and shame from our lives. We choose to live in Faith, Joy, and Peace. When we see this destructive pattern in ourselves or others, we kindly point it out and invite to move to the higher frequency of Love, Joy, and peace. | How do you manage when you have emotion of guilt or shame? |

In my businesses, we review one of the core ethos statements as a fun little 5-minute exercise each week. This keeps the ethos top of mind and gives us the opportunity to generate stories that build the culture.

Many of the same concepts of building a stable business culture with values also apply to family life. Building a stable and cohesive family unit takes intentional effort and dedication to shared values. Here are some exercises designed to help you reinforce these values within your family. These activities not only help in creating a strong family bond but also ensure that the values you hold dear are passed on to future generations.

## Exercise 1: Family Purpose Statement

**Objective:** Create or revisit your family purpose statement.
**Instructions:**

1. Gather all family members for a discussion.

2. Reflect on the values that are important to your family.

3. Write down a list of these values and what they mean to each member.

4. Combine these values into a cohesive mission statement.

5. Display the purpose statement in a prominent place in your home.

**Fun Stories Behind This Exercise:** Creating a family mission statement can lead to humorous and heartfelt moments as everyone shares their thoughts. It's a chance to hear stories from different perspectives and to understand what each member values most.

**Discussion Questions:**

➤ What values did they seem to hold above all others?

➤ What makes these items so meaningful?

## Exercise 2: Family Symbols and Heirlooms

**Objective:** Identify and discuss the significance of family symbols and heirlooms.

**Instructions:**

1. Ask each family member to bring an item that holds special meaning to them.

2. Share the story behind each item and why it is significant.

3. Discuss what these items symbolize about your family's history and values.

**Discussion Questions:**

➤ Are there any heirlooms in your family that have come to define and symbolize your ancestors?

➤ What special objects hold meaning to you?

➤ What did your ancestors stand for?

## Exercise 3: Family Values Worksheet

**Objective:** Reflect on and document your family's core values and experiences.

**Instructions:**

1. Each family member should complete the following questions individually.

2. Come together as a family to share and discuss your answers.

3. Create a family scrapbook or digital archive with everyone's responses.

**Discussion Questions:**

➤ Name five things your family enjoys doing together.

➤ What did these events mean to you?

➤ What does your family like to do for fun?

➤ What significant events have helped your family bond?

➤ What are some unique and defining life events that your family has been through?

## Exercise 4: Dream Gifts for Future Generations

**Objective:** Envision the legacy you want to leave for future generations.

**Instructions:**

1. Imagine you could wave a magic wand and bless your great-great-grandchildren with several gifts.

2. Write down what those gifts would be and why.

3. Discuss what you have learned from your ancestors that you want to pass on.

**Discussion Questions:**

➤ If you could wave a magic wand and bless your great-great-grandchildren or most loved ones with several gifts, what would they be?

➤ What is the greatest thing that you learned and was passed on to you from your ancestors?

These exercises are not only about documenting values and memories but also about creating meaningful interactions and shared experiences that strengthen family bonds. As you engage in these activities, you'll find that the values you hold dear will become more ingrained in your family's daily life, providing a stabilizing influence for generations to come.

**More on this can be found at: www.LegadoFamily.com**

# SUMMARY

In Chapter 3: Values—A Firm Foundation, we uncover the vital role values play, not just in business but in every facet of life. Initially focused on business, I now see values as the stabilizing force in personal, family, and public life. This chapter emphasizes how clarity in your core values eliminates confusion and creates a solid foundation. By embedding memorable stories and hang tags around these values, they become an active, vibrant part of your culture.

Think of values as the road system guiding you to success. Just like a family road trip is smoother on paved highways, having clear values keeps your organization on track. These values dictate behaviors, set the cultural tone, and ensure alignment with your core principles. Whether you're running a high-end restaurant valuing quality or a fast-food joint prioritizing speed, identifying and living by your values is crucial.

Through stories, this chapter shows how values shape your narrative. From a legendary football coach's consistent success to a mother's ability to raise self-reliant children despite economic hardships, these stories vividly demonstrate the power of clear values. These stories highlight how clear values guide actions, create a cohesive culture, and lead to long-term success. As we move forward, your strong, clear values will be the compass directing your first zig toward profitability.

CHAPTER 4

# ZIG NUMBER 1—DRIVE TO PROFITABILITY

As I revisit the principles from *The Zig Zag Principle* 12 years later, I'm amazed at how well the principles have stood the test of time. Of all the concepts in the book, the most vital to have a business sustain is getting to profitability.

In this revised edition, I'll update the modified Porter Model with more user-friendly graphics and introduce an amazing new tool titled "Where Do You Fish?" to ensure your business idea addresses a strong felt need. Additionally, I'll cover a third vital tool, the Value Decision Matrix, and wrap up the chapter with essential concepts like avoiding the rabbit syndrome, failing efficiently, and following the 80/20 rule.

Over the years, I've developed a successful process for starting a business. First, gather at least fifty ideas. Then, put them through three screening tools:

1. Where Do You Fish?

2. Porter Model (Rich Style)

3. Value Decision Matrix for the final 5-6 candidates.

Having a business idea is easy; determining if it's a good idea is the challenging part. These tools help refine high-potential ideas quickly. What's exciting is that these concepts have moved beyond theory—they've been tested, tried, and proven countless times.

Let's dive into Zig Number One: driving to profitability.

## ZIG NUMBER 1—DRIVE TO PROFITABILITY

When my wife and I first got married, we were both in school and broke. I had to take several jobs I wasn't all that excited about. I even had to work late-night shifts when I would have preferred being home because I instinctively knew I needed to do whatever it took to get to profitability. We tightened our budget, got a safe comfortable little basement apartment, and together worked our hearts out. We drove an old Dodge Colt that my wife's parents gave to us when we were married.

Our weekly food budget was $15-per-week. We lived off of potatoes and love. To justify our frugal lifestyle, I used to say, "We will live like you won't now, so we can live like you can't for the rest of our lives." At that stage, I hadn't given words to the idea of driving to profitability, but I instinctively understood its importance.

Whether you are starting out in life, starting a business, or are broke and starting over, your first zig always needs to take you toward profitability. Profitability means you're able to pay all your bills and have enough cash to move forward with your plans. It's easy to bypass this first step, given the ease of finding money, whether it's from a credit card, a government grant, a small business loan, or help from family. But at some point, the wells of easy cash will dry up, and you'll face a day of reckoning. If you don't have real cash coming in, you're going to be stopped dead in your tracks. So, don't let the easy allure of available cash sidetrack you from finding the path that will get you to that critical point of profitability.

This first zig requires sheer grit and raw determination. I often joke that when I am starting a new business, I will go out in the street and dance in a tutu if that is what it takes to get to profitability. While my efforts have never come to that, I will do what it takes, within the framework of my values, to get enough cash to move forward. Operating from the black gives you a much higher level of confidence and a sense of durability that you can't have if you're always worrying about draining your bank account. If you have money in the bank or cash in your pocket, you can breathe a sigh of relief as you keep trying different things until you get one of your ideas to work. And if you can't get an idea to be profitable, then check it off your list and try something different.

This is what I call failing efficiently, which we'll discuss in more detail later in the chapter.

Just before the dot.com bubble burst in the early 2000s, I was working as the general manager of a company called MyJobSearch.com. It was a heavily funded business in the Web 1.0 Internet bubble phase. This was a wild and crazy time when companies were being built and funded by people writing business plans on paper napkins. This company had hired forty or fifty employees, and we didn't even know what the exact product was that we were building. And because we were living on investment bankers' money, we had no clue how we were ever going to get to profitability. Heck, we didn't need to!

When the bubble burst, everything imploded. Not just for this company but for almost every other company in the web industry. The reason this company and those other companies failed was because they were not built for profitability. We had never needed to pursue that strategy. In fact, during this time, the strategy for most of these companies was to get an IPO and then get bought up by a bigger company. But, as countless people who lost huge sums of money found out, that is not a business plan that can be sustained.

So many businesses I've seen think that all they have to do is head straight for that beacon in the fog. It doesn't work. The first zig always needs to be to get cash!

## FINDING HIDDEN ASSETS

When I am starting a business, the first question I ask myself is, "What skills do I have that can get me to profitability the fastest?"

This question should be asked whether we're trying to build a business or any other part of our life. The answer doesn't have to be perfectly aligned with your beacon in the fog, just something that is close enough and is an inch or two up from where you currently are. Remember, we're zigzagging.

When my business partner and I started CastleWave, I had a knack (for which I had been well paid) for getting keywords to the top of the search engines on the Internet. I had sworn I would not share any of my search engine optimization (SEO) secrets and mental knowledge with other people because I was done making other people rich, and I was in the mode of creating my own businesses. But in the earliest days of CastleWave, I realized that the fastest way to cash was to fill the need other companies had for SEO work. I had some contacts in New York City who I knew wanted to get their own websites to the top of the search engines. My business partner and I flew to New York and sold these contacts on search engine optimization. We were almost instantly profitable because I was willing to do what I regarded as the equivalent of going out in the street and dancing in a tutu. I did not initially do what I wanted to do; instead, I zigged to the fastest source of cash I could identify because I understood how important that first zig is.

## MINIMIZE YOUR RISKS

I once worked with some individuals who operated a very successful insurance practice. They had a great business financially, but they were utterly uninspired by what they were doing. They were not moving toward their beacon in the fog in any part of their life, and they were frustrated—not to mention running on fumes. At the same time, they had a great idea for a very progressive technology. That was where their true passion was. They knew they had something good and had even started filing the patent for their idea.

The problem was that every time they started down the path and began to make some progress, they would shift into panic mode. I could actually see the anxiety and pressure building up in their faces and their eyes. As I did some digging to understand what was holding them back, I finally was able to find out what was going on. They were worried their business model might not work. They would get partway down the path and then just freeze. They were afraid of failure. They knew so many entrepreneurs who had done the equivalent of running to Vegas and putting everything on black—and most of the time, they had failed. Then they would head home broke and deal with lives that had been ruined.

When I finally understood what was holding them back, I said, "Listen, you don't have to bet the farm. You don't have to give away your soul. You don't have to risk everything you value and believe in to succeed as an entrepreneur. There is a better way. It's okay to use your insurance business as a base and then zigzag to success." I then outlined the steps they should take. It was as if someone had pulled a huge, sopping wet blanket off of them. They got so excited. The fear left their eyes, and their faces lit up. And soon they were zigzagging toward their beacon in the fog.

## THE NEED FOR PACING

From my own experiences, I have found that when people set

their beacon in the fog and then head directly toward it without zigzagging, one of three things will occur:

1. **They never do it.** There are lots of people who talk and talk about their dream and what they are going to do; but then, before they've taken their first step, their knees shake and wobble, and they don't dare take the risk needed to progress toward their goal. I used to think these people were just weak-hearted, but I've decided that subconsciously they realize there is a chance they may fail, so they do not even start.

2. **They run out of resources and fail.** The second group of people race toward their goal full speed ahead, and when they get halfway there, they run out of resources and fail.

3. **They miss the target.** The third group runs straight toward their goal, but by the time they get there, the target has completely moved, and their great idea is now a lost opportunity. In many cases, if they had taken their blinders off and looked from side to side occasionally, they would have seen the need to adjust their course.

Zigzagging deliberately toward your goal makes the going slower. It is more methodical and might seem harder, especially for those of us who lack patience. But there is a much higher chance of success because zigzagging allows you to inch toward your goal and then adjust and adapt until you actually get to viability.

One of the benefits of this approach is that it puts you in a mindset of abundance by setting parameters for what you can and can't risk or lose. And when that happens, you find yourself free from the fear of scarcity, which tends to paralyze us rather than motivate us. An example of this approach is found in the success story of the Marriott Corporation. In the 1920s, J. Willard Marriott opened a nine-stool A&W Root Beer stand in Washington, D.C. As time went on, he realized that people bought lots of root beer in the hot summer months but not so much during winter. So, he started selling soup as well and changed the name to The Hot Shoppe. In the early days, he and his partners worked lots of long hours to get their shop to profitability. As they looked for additional opportunities, they obtained the food service management contract with the U.S. Department of Treasury. Then during World War II, The Hot Shoppe catered to the many defense people who moved to the nation's capital.

It wasn't until 1957 that Bill Marriott opened his first hotel. As the business grew, he found parallel opportunities as his company grew into one of the largest hotel chains in the world. Some of those ventures included expanding the food business to service major airlines and buying additional restaurants like Bob's Big Boy. With each new project, Bill was able to get enough cash to move on to his bigger goals. This is a great example of a company starting small and zigzagging its way up to long-term strength and success.

Many first businesses revolve around services. The reason is that service businesses can usually get you to cash quickly. The downside is that they are often labor-intensive in the beginning. At the early stage, you are literally the butcher, the baker, and the candlestick maker all rolled into one because you typically don't have any (or many) employees, and so you have to carry the brunt of the work.

For example, when we started CastleWave, my business partner and I had to be the salespeople to land our first account in New York. I then had to be the programmer and had to personally optimize the website. We also had to be the secretary and bookkeeper and take care of billing and collecting the money. This was very time-consuming work, but it did bring in the first bursts of cash that allowed CastleWave to get off the ground.

## GETTING IDEAS FOR YOUR FIRST ZIG

The question that is asked of me as an entrepreneur more than any other question is: "Hey, I've got this really cool idea. What do you think? Is this viable? Will it get me to cash?" Coming up with an idea is the easy part. The harder part is figuring out what is a good idea and what is a bad idea. When deciding what business to build, I always start with at least 50 business ideas. I then run the ideas through the following sequence of tools to determine what idea should be turned into a business.

Tool number one is *Where Do You Fish?* Tool two is the *Porter Model* based on Michael E. Porter's *Five Forces Competitive Position Model.* By this point, I have narrowed the good ideas down to four to six ideas. The final tool I use to determine which idea to create a business on is the *Value Decision Matrix.*

# TOOL #1 WHERE DO YOU FISH?

## Be a Catcherman (or Catcherwoman), Not a Fisherman (or Fisherwoman)

The "Where Do You Fish?" model uses a fun fishing analogy to break down market strategies into four key quadrants: The Mud Puddle, The Swamp, The Ocean, and The Fish Hatchery. Each quadrant represents a unique combination of market size and felt need, guiding you on where to reel in your business efforts. The big takeaway here is that you'll get your business off the ground and sales will skyrocket if you're meeting your customers' felt needs head-on.

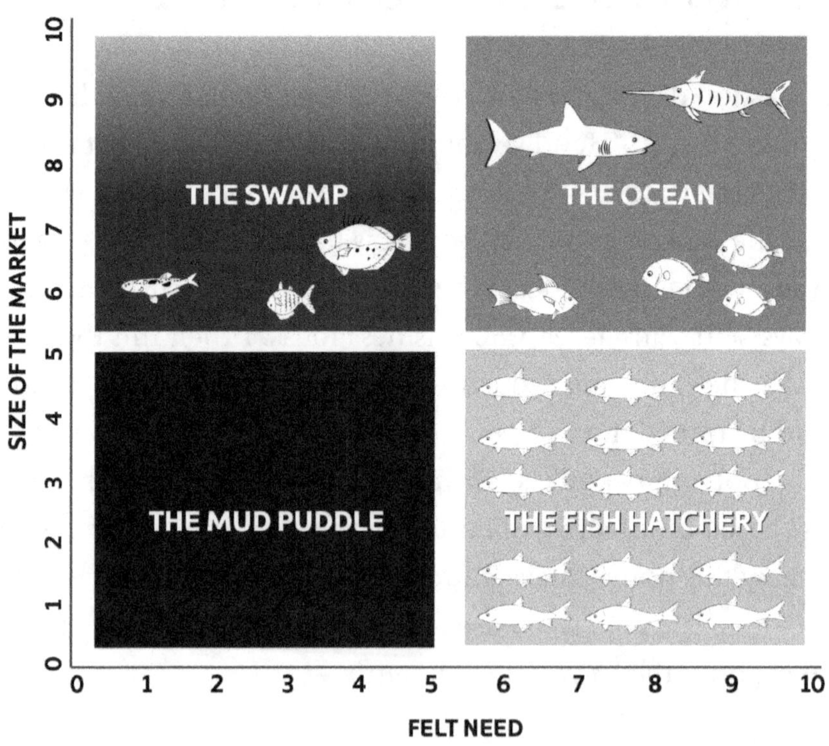

### ➤ **The Mud Puddle:** Small Market with Low Need

**The Mud Puddle** is a sad, murky place with a tiny market and low felt need. This is the last place you want to start your business because, well, there are no fish to catch!

*Business Example:* A Pencil Sorter

Picture a company that creates a super exciting, super high-tech pencil sorter. This amazing gadget sorts your pencils and pens with just one push of a button—by size, color, or even by how much ink and graphite is left in them. Cool, huh? But who really cares? The felt need for a pencil/pen sorter is practically nonexistent. Despite its innovative design, the product flops because there aren't enough potential customers. The company struggles to make sales and eventually sinks. Fish don't live in mud puddles, and neither do your customers.

### ➤ **The Swamp:** Large Market with Low Need

The Swamp is a big, stagnant market with low felt need. It's filled with yucky fish like carp and catfish—low-value and undesirable. Products here often end up in discount bins or clearance sales because people just don't care enough to buy them.

*Business Example:* Cleaning Supplies with Matching Scents

Imagine a company that creates a line of cleaning supplies with matching scents—like a toilet bowl cleaner that matches the scent of your bleach. Great idea, right? But at the end of the day, how many people lie awake at night dreaming of a perfectly matching bathroom scent? The market is large, but the felt need is low. This business would struggle with low margins and require tons of marketing to convince customers that their product is relevant. In the Swamp, the fish aren't tasty, and neither are the business opportunities.

➤ **The Ocean:** Large Market with High Barriers

The Ocean is a vast market with high felt need, but it's full of challenges. First of all, most of the Ocean is just water, not fish. Fishing here requires a big boat and expensive gear, much like launching a business in a competitive, well-established industry. It takes tons of marketing dollars to even play here. Startups often drown because they can't compete with the big fish. Additionally, there are sharks and whales, and small businesses that start here are shark bait. Most of the whales that live here, like Amazon, actually started in the Fish Hatchery.

*Business Example:* Consumer Electronics

Entering the consumer electronics market, like launching a new smartphone, is a classic case of fishing in the Ocean. Demand is high, and the market is huge, but giants like Apple and Samsung rule these waters. A new player needs massive investment in tech, marketing, and distribution to even stand a chance. Most startups get lost at sea before they can make a splash. Small fish get eaten by the big ones in the Ocean.

➤ **The Fish Hatchery:** Constrained Market with High Need

The Fish Hatchery is the dream spot to start your business. It's a smaller, constrained market with a high felt need. Here, the fish are hungry and eager for what you're offering. This quadrant is perfect for a new business to thrive because there's strong demand and a manageable market size for targeted marketing and customer engagement.

*Business Example:* Social Interaction Services during COVID-19

Imagine a startup that helps grandparents get visits and social interaction during the COVID-19 pandemic. The market is focused on elderly people isolated due to health concerns, but the felt need is sky-high. By facilitating safe and meaningful social interactions through virtual visits or carefully managed in-person protocols, this business meets a deep emotional need. Or think about a service that brings pain relief, normalcy, and joy to terminally ill children. These services cater to a small, specific market but address incredibly strong needs, leading to high engagement and loyalty. This is the essence of the Fish Hatchery: addressing powerful felt needs in a focused market, driving natural sales and deep customer connection.

Knowing where to fish in the business world can make or break your success. Steer clear of the Mud Puddle and the Swamp, where markets are too small or felt need too low. Be cautious of the Ocean, where competition is fierce and resources are essential. Instead, cast your line in the Fish Hatchery, where a strong felt need and a manageable market size provide the best conditions for growth. Always aim to push clients down and to the right in the model: toward smaller markets with stronger felt need. This strategy helps you reel in viable, profitable, and loyal customers, leading to long-term success. Start in the Fish Hatchery, build your business, and then expand your horizons. By meeting your customers' felt needs and ramping up urgency through smart marketing, you'll create a loyal customer base and keep your business thriving.

# TOOL #2 – MODIFIED PORTER MODEL

The second tool that I use when I am vetting ideas is my modified version of a "Porter Model" based on Michael E. Porter's *Five Forces Competitive Position Model*.

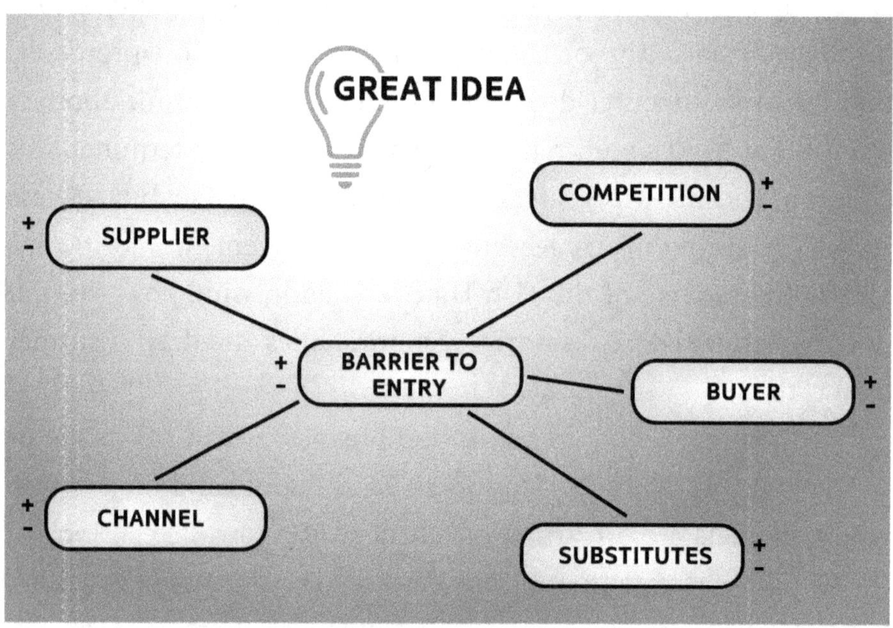


In my model, there are six factors to look at:

1. **Barrier to Entry**
   - How difficult is it to enter this market space?
   - Do you have an advantage over the competition?
   - Once in, how do you keep others out of the space?

## 2. Supplier

- How much power do you have over the suppliers?
- Are there multiple suppliers available?
- Can you get a better price on your supplies than the competition?

## 3. Substitutes

- Is there a feature of your product or service that would compel customers to buy your product over the competition's product?
- Is there a substitute that will compete with your product?

## 4. Buyer

- What is the bargaining power of the buyers? Do your target buyers have the power to force the price of your product down?
- Can you command a premium price for your product?

## 5. Competition

- Who is competing for market share in your product? Is the market saturated?
- Is there a rivalry among competitors in the industry? Note that competition can be a good thing unless it squashes your chances of entering the market.

## 6. Channel

- Do you have access to a distribution channel? Channel is probably the most important of all the factors. If there is not a market need for your product and a way to get it to the customer, then your business will fail. In the businesses I create, I will not move forward until I have fully figured out the channel. Most people think they will build the product, then try to sell it. The correct order is to ensure that the market will buy your product, then determine how you will deliver it to your customers and only then go ahead and build it.
- Do you know who is going to buy your product or service?

For each factor, you will come up with several questions similar to what I have posed above. The answer to each question will receive a positive (+), a negative (–), or a neutral (o) result, ending in a final overall score for each factor. As you look at the positives and negatives of your business idea, you will be able to see rather clearly if it is an idea that works or just a pipe dream.

## TOOL #3 THE VALUE DECISION MATRIX

Fifteen years ago, I developed a powerful tool that helps individuals make complex decisions and get to clarity quickly. The tool is called the Value Decision Matrix. This is always the final tool that I run on the final four to six business ideas that I narrow down after having used *Where Do You Fish* and the *Porter Model.*

This tool not only helps you identify and rank your core

values, foresee conflicts, and communicate effectively to resolve them, and by weighing values and scoring options, it brings order to chaos, boosts confidence, and allows both logical and intuitive thinking. Plus, it saves time and energy by guiding you toward what's truly important.

My wife and I, as well as all the individuals I mentor, use it for all major decisions in our lives. And now, I want to share this tool with you. Whether you're facing a major crossroads or simply looking to live with more intention and integrity, this tool will help you cut through the noise and make decisions with confidence and clarity.

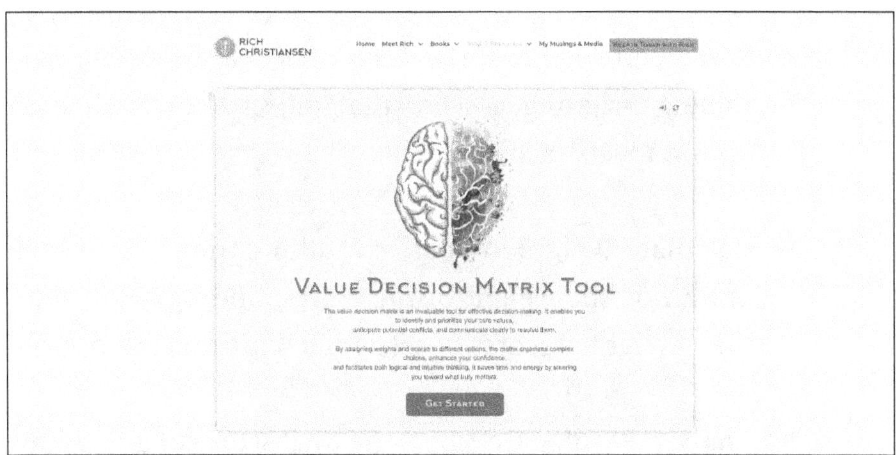


I believe that when we connect with our values and make choices that honor our highest selves, we tap into a source of power and purpose that can transform our lives and the world around us. The Value Decision Matrix is invaluable for effective decision-making. It enables you to identify and prioritize your core values, anticipate potential conflicts, and communicate clearly to resolve them. It does this by having you assign weights and scores to different options. .

Here's a breakdown of how it works:

➤ **Identify Core Values:** Begin by listing your core values or criteria crucial for the decision.

➤ **List Options:** Compile a list of all possible options or alternatives you are considering.

➤ **Assign Weights:** Assign a weight to each core value based on its importance.

➤ **Score Options:** Evaluate each option against your core values, assigning a score that reflects how well each option meets each value.

➤ **Calculate Weighted Scores:** Multiply the score of each option by the weight of the corresponding value. Sum these weighted scores to get a total score for each option.

➤ **Analyze Results:** Compare the total scores of all options to identify the best choice based on your values.

This process ensures a comprehensive evaluation of all factors, helping you make well-rounded decisions.

I would strongly encourage you to use the free tool that I have create online. https://richchristiansen.com/value-decision-matrix-tool/ The image below does not include the logic, the calculating of the score, or the weighting of the values.

| | Value Consideration | Value 1 | Value 2 | Value 3 | Value 4 | Value 5 | Value 6 | Value 7 | Value 8 | Value 9 | Value 10 |
|---|---|---|---|---|---|---|---|---|---|---|---|
| | Person XXX | | | | | | | | | | |
| | Person YYY | | | | | | | | | | |
| | Value Weighted Score | 1.00 | 1.00 | 1.00 | 1.00 | 1.00 | 1.00 | 1.00 | 1.00 | 1.00 | |
| | Value Capacity Score | | | | | | | | | | |
| Idea or Concept | | Value 1 | Value 2 | Value 3 | Value 4 | Value 5 | Value 6 | Value 7 | Value 8 | Value 9 | Value 10 |
| Option 1 | | | | | | | | | | | |
| Option 2 | | | | | | | | | | | |
| Option 3 | | | | | | | | | | | |
| Option 4 | | | | | | | | | | | |
| Option 5 | | | | | | | | | | | |
| Option 6 | | | | | | | | | | | |
| Option 7 | | | | | | | | | | | |
| Option 8 | | | | | | | | | | | |
| Option 9 | | | | | | | | | | | |
| Option 10 | | | | | | | | | | | |

# AVOID THE RABBIT SYNDROME

As you look for ideas, there are a couple of things you should remember to avoid. The first is what I refer to as "the rabbit syndrome." Some people see ideas popping out everywhere they look. They'll spot a great idea or concept and proclaim, "Look! A rabbit!" Then they see another and another and another (if you've spent any time in rabbit country, you know they're everywhere). They chase one rabbit after another and end up so busy chasing every rabbit that pops up that they never actually drive to profitability. At some point, you have to settle on one rabbit and chase it as hard as you can—hopefully to a successful end.

Another mistake you want to avoid is falling in love with an idea to the point where you can't see its deficiencies. In 1989, I contributed my fair share to making my first $2 million business mistake. I keep the reminder front and center on my life-trophy shelf to remind me never to make this mistake again.

So, what was it we made? We did what so many eager

engineering types do—we built a way cool, exciting, leading-edge product (in this case, a digital power line transmission device) and then tried to sell it. In our engineering minds, we just knew customers would buy these boxes by the truckloads. We had attended the trade shows and been mobbed by fellow engineers who thought our idea was awesome, which convinced us this product was going to be a barn burner. Everyone told us we were so smart, and this was the coolest technology ever.

Well, cool technology does not necessarily lead to actual customers, and in 1990, the company went belly up! Why? Because our product did exactly what a $20 power cable could do, only our box cost $995. And, in our zeal, we engineers never stopped to consider that, if given the choice, people would opt for the $20 cable, even though our technology was "better."

And, lest you think engineers are the only ones who get too focused on their great ideas, I have an associate who has a fervent desire to promote ultra-modern cement homes. He has wanted to create a business around these buildings because he is passionate about the benefits they provide. Indeed, the concept and these homes are amazing. The only problem is that he lives in a community where the homes are built using wood, bricks, stucco, and traditional architecture. In spite of his efforts, the people in his community have not caught on to his vision of building cement homes. You do not want to create a product in which consumers have no interest because if you don't have a channel to sell your products through, your business will fail.

I have learned time and again it is best to sell it then build it rather than build it and sell it.

# HOW MUCH CASH DO I NEED?

I define profitability as having enough money to cover "the nut" and having a buffer that will allow me to move on to the next zag. Everyone has different needs, or "nuts," so profitability will be different for each person or each business. I am covering the nut in my personal life when I have enough money to pay all my expenses, such as housing, utilities, recreation, food, clothing, education needs, health insurance, and a little more to take care of those unexpected extras that always crop up.

If a family makes a budget and keeps track of how much it costs to live each month, then that is the family's monthly nut. In business, the nut would include the building, utilities, the cost of doing business, payroll for any employees, and any other expenses it takes to run the business, including paying yourself. (If you forget that, you'll destroy the nut in your personal life.) Any amount over these expenses is profit. You need to carefully calculate what it's going to cost you to get to profitability. This can't be a number you guess at. It needs to be a firm number and one that you write down.

# COMPONENTS OF ZIG NUMBER 1

Because your first zig is so important, I want to dissect its components and look at each one individually.

> ➤ **Financial Number:** Zig number 1 is a financial number. You have to have a financial target number specifying how much you want to bring in. Refer back to the nut

you determined in the last section.

➤ **Allocation of Time:** How much time are you going to dedicate to getting to cash? How long will you give yourself to achieve this financial target? I will typically dedicate 65 percent of my resources toward getting to profitability, 30 percent toward zag number 2, and 5 percent toward zig number 3. And, as I look ahead, I never plan beyond three zigzags.

➤ **Duration of Time:** How long are you willing to run at this pace? Anyone can sprint for a block or two. But what reserves do you have if you end up needing to run a marathon?

➤ **Financial Target:** What is your target for the profit you want to make? How and why is this different from the financial number above? After you have covered the nut, what is your goal for how much profit you want to make?

➤ **Financial Resources:** How much in the way of financial resources are you willing to invest? How do you want to allocate your financial resources? In the early days of entrepreneurship, I used to be more willing to mortgage my house or use my emergency buffer to help fund my businesses. Now I have a policy: I absolutely will not mortgage my house or dip into my safety net. We will talk more about this in Chapter 7 when we talk about guardrails.

➤ **Relationship Capital:** We have already talked about relationship capital in Chapter 1. Think carefully about how much relationship capital you want to use when driving to profitability. One of the reasons I choose not to sell to my close family and friends is because I am not willing to expend all my relationship capital in one fell swoop. It is important in the early stages of your business not to drain your whole relationship bank account. Selectively choose a few key individuals who can help you, but carefully define and limit how much relationship capital you're willing to spend. Then make sure you give those people a "thank you" and put something back into their relationship bank account. Gratitude goes a long way with relationship capital.

➤ **Give Yourself Permission to Be Miserable:** I'll be honest; this is not an easy stage. Sometimes, in getting to cash, I have to do a lot of things I really don't like doing. I have to do the books, answer the phone calls, and open the mail. I do it all! I can do it; I just don't like to do it. So, I give myself permission to be miserable and endure—but only for so long.

## RESOURCE LIST

To help you quantify your responses to these questions, here's a worksheet that will help you see in black and white the road you're considering heading down. Use the results from your Value Equation to help populate this worksheet.

| Resource List |
|---|
| How much money do you have to put toward this project?<br><br>$ _______________ |
| How much time each week are you able or willing to dedicate to this project?<br><br>_______________hours |
| How long of a timeframe Do you have to work with?<br><br>_______________months/years |
| Emotionally, how long can you give yourself to accomplish this goal?<br><br>_______________months/years |
| How much pain (emotional, financial, relationship, time) are you willing to endure? |

## THE 80/20 RULE

During this first zig, it is important to remember that you are not going to have time to be perfect at everything. Many people who are perfectionists or have a methodical personality type fail at this stage because they try to be great and have everything perfect and buttoned up. You need to think, instead, about the 80/20 rule. In general, 20 percent of the effort yields 80 percent of the results. The key to success is not to do anything that isn't geared towards the 80 percent success ratio. You're not striving for perfection. You're striving for profitability.

I often say that competence and incompetence always rear their heads. But it is important during this time to know those things where competency is a must. If you produce a shoddy product, then your customers will never use you again. But, as you do so, you do not need the perfect organization or to micromanage all the details. During this phase, the important 20 percent is providing a quality product and getting to cash. If your office is a mess or you haven't taken the trash out in a week, take a deep breath and give yourself a break. You can get to those things later.

On the other hand, it is imperative that you keep track of your books and know what your bottom line is, but don't stress about the little things as you take care of the big ones. I have a former business associate who had the mantra on his desk to "Strive for Mediocrity." He was a perfectionist in every area of his life. If he saw a "t" that needed to be crossed or an "i" that needed to be dotted, he would take whatever time it took to stress over minor details. He soon found he could not be effective living this way. He had to look at the bigger picture and choose which things he needed to focus on to succeed and then let go of the minor things. He was trying to be more "mediocre" in the smaller details so that he could shine in the important aspects of the business. One of my business partners used to call this "selective negligence." He would selectively neglect the less important things so that he could achieve the bigger goals. Once we became profitable and got to the next zag of adding resources, we could hire someone to take care of those small details.

This can be applied whether you are an individual trying to accomplish an important project with your family, a small bootstrap company, or a large corporation. You can apply this same principle to a new division you may be heading up or to a new product or a new service you may be launching in a large corporation. Your budget may be bigger, but the principles will make the division or large corporation even stronger.

## FAIL EFFICIENTLY

I've learned a great deal over the years about failing efficiently. When I use the word fail, I'm not talking about falling off tall buildings, going bankrupt, or losing everything. What I mean by failing efficiently is that if you can't get to profitability, you need to accept that you have nowhere left to go. You have to become financially profitable before you go on to the next step. I see far too many people say, "Oh, well, if I just add resources and scale, then I'll get to profitability!" But they are inevitably wrong.

Failing efficiently means that unless you hit profitability in whatever time you've allocated, you are done! You need to stop. If you do, you've failed efficiently and life goes on. If you aren't willing to stop, you will fail at a level that may have devastating consequences.

In your personal life, if you keep going into debt without getting to profitability, you will end up in financial ruin. You cannot keep trying to add resources or buy more and more things unless you have the cash to pay for them. (And while, yes, credit can be easy to get, at some point you'll max out, and no one will loan you more money.) Become profitable in your life, in whatever pursuit you have undertaken.

## SUMMARY

When you are driving to profitability in zig number 1, follow the basic components. Set a financial target and figure out how long you will allow yourself to hit your target. And be sure to give yourself permission to be miserable along the way. This is hard work, and you'll have to dig down deep to get through it. But absolutely do not start working on the other steps until you hit this first zig. If you fail, that's fine. You failed efficiently. You can restart. You should absolutely begin your undertaking with the mindset that you are going to succeed, but if you don't, get past the pain and move on to the next thing. However, as your first step, always drive for profitability as your zig number 1.

CHAPTER 5

# ZAG NUMBER 2—ADDING PROCESSES AND RESOURCES

I love the Taj Mahal. I've had the good fortune to visit this remarkable shrine several times, and neither words nor pictures can describe it. What adds to its magnificence is that I've always come straight from the chaos of India, where there is mayhem everywhere, which makes approaching into this peaceful grove is like walking into another world.

The Taj Mahal was built with a labor force of over twenty

thousand workers recruited from all across northern India and other parts of the region. In addition to common laborers, the workforce included sculptors from Bukhara, calligraphers from Syria and Persia, inlayers from southern India, and stonecutters from Baluchistan. A team of thirty-seven men formed the creative unit. Of these, one was a specialist in carving marble flowers and another was the best at building turrets. It took twenty years to complete the Taj Mahal. It was built by Mughal Emperor Shah Jahan in memory of his beloved third wife Mumtaz Mahal. It is considered one of the most beautiful buildings in the world and is a symbol of eternal love.

Imagine for a moment the possibility of this emperor trying to build the Taj Mahal all by himself. He clearly had a vision of what it was to be. He was a very wealthy man, so he had the necessary cash. And likely he knew where to find the materials from which this edifice was constructed. Despite all that he had at his disposal, building the Taj Mahal would have been an impossible feat, even if Shah Jahan had several lifetimes in which to complete the work.

Instead, he put together his beacon in the fog, fueled it with his passion, and then added resources—lots and lots of resources. And as he added those resources, he had to get everyone to catch the same vision so they could complete something that beautiful.

## ADDING RESOURCES

In the first zig, you made your business or your life profitable. Zag number 2 is about adding resources. Once you have enough cash from the first zig, you can use it to add the people, equipment, and other resources that you need. You need to do so in order to help perform the labor-intensive work that keeps the cash flowing. Then you can spend more of your time defining the processes and adding meat to the bones of your organization. This is the time to formalize, structure, and expand those things that led you to your initial success in zig number 1.

Getting to cash feels great! Your determination has begun to bear fruit. You're in the black. Life is good. You're actually making money. The only problem is you're completely worn out. And your gas tank is now on fumes, if not completely empty. You know you need to make a change, but you're also sensing how hard it is going to be to let go of some of your control and bring others on board. Doing so requires that you shift gears dramatically, and if you don't, you'll never get to your destination.

Adding resources is harder than it sounds, but it's the only way you'll build your dream. I have a neighbor who owns a shoe repair shop. This man makes a decent living and takes care of his family's basic needs. However, to keep his head above water, he has to work day after day, week after week, repairing those shoes single-handedly. If he needs a day off, he has to close the shop. Same if he's under the weather or has to take care of a sick wife or child. Of course, that leads to a loss of income. Now, his business model allows for some days off, but it's a pretty thin margin. If something major happened, the effects could be catastrophic.

My friend has made it through zig number 1 profitability—but he has not thought to turn his skis in the other direction for zag number 2. In other words, he has not added the resources that would allow him to live a fuller, richer, and safer life.

A key reason many people have a hard time adding resources

is they have become accustomed to micromanaging every aspect of their business. As hard as it can be to let go of control, as you hire the right people to fill in the gaps of knowledge or skill that you don't have, and then as you help them learn your processes, your company will begin to reach its full potential. Think of yourself as being akin to Emperor Shah Jahan, who may not have known how to carve flowers out of stone but was able to hire someone to do that job—and thus help him create his masterpiece.

I'm familiar with a family-owned business, run by a father and his sons, where the father has micromanaged every aspect of the business. The father is now getting old and is about to retire. He has talented sons who want to modernize the business, but his response is always, "We have been doing business this way for over forty years. This is how it has to be done." When the sons bring up the need to modernize equipment or processes, the father adamantly refuses.

It's no wonder the sons and their families are frustrated. They feel stuck in a business that is archaic, and they would like a little leeway in bringing the business into the computer age and making it more productive.

This example is common among family-run businesses, but the same plight is apparent among businesses founded by a strong-minded personality, who is then unwilling to bring in additional resources and let them do what they were hired to do. As you begin to take zag number 2 in order to grow your business, remembering that it is all about discipline will help you loosen your grip on the controls. The image I keep in mind to help me do this (because, I'll admit it, I can be a bit controlling) is what I call the "Yes, Yes, Yes, NO! Principle." While you are working on zig number 1 and trying to get to cash, you will, of necessity, say "Yes" to many things, such as:

➤ Yes, I will do the accounting.

➤ Yes, I will sell a small order that has potential for larger orders.

➤ Yes, I will answer the phones.

➤ Yes, I will take out the trash.

➤ No, I will not compromise my values.

➤ Now, as you add resources, it's time to add a few more "Nos." Some of these might be:

➤ No, I will not take out the trash. I will hire a cleaning person.

➤ No, I will not do my own accounting. I will outsource my taxes to an accountant.

➤ No, I will not answer the phones and do the bookkeeping. I will hire an administrative assistant.

# HIRING SMART IN A GLOBALIZED, REMOTE WORK ENVIRONMENT

As you add resources to your business or your life, you still need to keep your cash flow heading in the right direction. Obviously, you don't want to begin hiring if doing so is going to put you in the red. But as you hire, you need to be clear in your mind, and with those you hire, that if the business becomes less profitable, you will have to decrease resources. This may seem harsh, but if you have employees in your organization who are not getting you to cash, it puts the whole company at risk. It is better to lay off those people who are not performing or creating value so you can create opportunities for more employees in the long run.

I was a middle manager in a company that hired a lot of employees but did not become profitable. That company waited until it was completely out of money and had declared bankruptcy before telling the employees they were out of jobs. To add insult, the employees were let go without being paid for their last month of work. Blind bliss is not bliss at all. It would have been much better for every person in that company to have been laid off when the problems started so they could begin their new job search, rather than wasting a month doing work for which they would never be paid.

In your life, you have to do the same thing. When you get to cash, you can spend a little more money adding resources such as a house, a car, a computer, or just some things that will make your life nicer and more efficient. When times get tight, you need to immediately tighten your budget and stop adding those resources. If times get really tight, you might have to sell off that nice car to make ends meet. The key is to always keep a close eye on your bottom line. Always stay profitable.

If you're creative as you think about adding resources, you may be able to make more progress and spend less money. When we began to add resources to our company, the first significant hires were not college graduates. They were not even college students; they were nerdy sixteen- and seventeen-year-old high school boys. In our drive to profitability, I needed to add the resource of engineers. I knew I couldn't afford to hire engineers at the going rate, and I also knew I could train people who had a working knowledge of computers and the Internet to do what needed to be done. It hit me one day that my labor force could be found among my teenaged sons' friends. My only concern was that I needed them to have a strong vision, so I told them, "When you walk in this door each day, you're no longer seventeen. You're an MBA graduate from Harvard, and I expect you to behave like one." And guess what? They did exactly that. They grasped what I needed them to do, and they bought into the company culture. It probably didn't hurt that we paid them far more than they could have earned flipping burgers, but for a number of strategic reasons, those kids were so excited to come to work, they would sleep on the couch some nights because they were totally vested in what we were trying to do.

On the flipside, at this same time I made a couple of horrific hires, in part because we didn't have our value system clearly in place. During this time, I was literally living off three to four hours of sleep a night. I hired an executive assistant who had a good resume, but what impressed me even more were her outstanding grades and recommendations. I had some concern that her work experience was a bit thin; but I needed someone quickly, so I hired her assuming her grades indicated a solid work ethic.

One week while my business partner and I were working a trade show in Florida, I kept trying to call into my office. I tried at several different times, but I just could not make contact with my new assistant. I finally called another recent hire who was supposed to be at the office. She did call me right back and said she was on a short lunch break and would call me back, which she failed to do. After four days of not being able to reach anyone, I called my wife and asked if she would go by the office and find out what was going on. When she arrived, the front door was locked and all of the lights were off. She found the main telephone was set to voice message. She did find an engineer in a back room, where he was working on a project. When she asked him what was going on, he told her that these two women, who were supposed to be answering my phones and greeting people, had decided that since I was gone that they would "work from home" (before that was a thing) that week.

Needless to say, I had to terminate both these women when I returned from my business trip. I made the mistake of hiring two young women who weren't hungry for the work I offered and who had a safety net at home that would rescue them. I also made the mistake of not screening them effectively against my organizational values, one of which is that we value hard workers.

Since that experience, I have learned to not be too busy to pay close attention as I add resources. I've also developed a series of questions and skills assessments that I run potential hires through, especially my executive admin, who I believe is my most important hire.

Other Resources to Add: Your organization will need resources other than more people. Resources can include more capital or a new piece of equipment that will simplify your processes. For example, if I were to create a cookie company, once I made enough money selling my mixes, I would look at buying a commercial mixer that does all the work of mixing the dough and then another one that cuts the cookies—after looking carefully at their cost and the potential return on my investment.

Outsourcing is another way to add resources. I started a company a decade ago with one of my sons. My son created a website, and we then outsourced the task of building five or six more websites. We gave the developer our website template and told her exactly how we wanted our sites to be built. Then we focused on other more lucrative parts of the venture.

One good thing about outsourcing is that you don't have to worry as much about the value system. The high production or the end result is what matters when you outsource. The key to outsourcing is that you only want to outsource those things that can be thrown over the wall to someone who can do them independently. Do not try to outsource those things that require your full involvement. For example, I would not want to outsource my company's financial books. There are so many moving parts in my books that my executive assistant and I must go through them daily. I want to know when bills go out, when we will be paid, and when our bills are due.

One time I tried to outsource one of my companies' bookkeeping to someone I knew in town. It ended up being a nightmare because I was no longer able to know at a moment's notice exactly where I stood financially. On the other hand, I do outsource my payroll. We send the payroll agency the hours each of my employees work, and they take care of all the required forms and paperwork. I also outsource my taxes to my accountant. We just send him a copy of our QuickBooks and the year-end papers, and he can take care of our taxes without taking any of my time.

## A NEW ANALOGY FOR TODAY'S WORLD

Imagine pulling up to your favorite fast-food joint. You're hungry, you've got your order ready, but the person at the drive-up window suddenly locks the window and takes a walk around the parking lot. Your business comes to a standstill. No matter how advanced our technology gets, some things still need a human touch.

In our modern, remote work environment, this analogy underscores the importance of having reliable, engaged team members. Even with tools like Upwork allowing us to engage talent globally—from my executive admin in the Philippines to my senior engineer in Pakistan—consistent, dedicated customer service is crucial. The next renaissance of business will revolve around exceptional customer service, and ensuring that our virtual team members are aligned with our values and committed to their roles is key to maintaining that standard.

In this context, hiring smart means not only looking for skills but also for the right fit with your company culture and values, ensuring that everyone, no matter where they are in the world, is pulling in the same direction.

## BUILDING PROCESSES

Now that you've started bringing in some cash and adding resources, your organization is going to need more structure and discipline.

As you add more flesh to the bones of your infrastructure, you'll need to work on making consistent progression. This will require that you build on what you have learned so far as you have been driving to profitability. In some cases, those will be lessons you haven't even realized you've learned.

I hate the technical term "Standard Operating Procedures" and how boring it sounds. I had one person I am mentoring begin calling it "the source of all truth." The entire perception and excitement level in her company shifted when she started doing this.

Consistency is what people purchase, and this step and part of the zigzag process will:

➤ Take the pressure off you

➤ Create consistency

➤ Set you on the path for a higher multiple exit

These operating guides and being well documented is one of the key things purchasers of business look at.

Building processes for your organization is vital to your short-term and long-term viability. It's a step that often gets overlooked as you head toward your beacon in the fog, but I've been convinced of its importance since I was a kid mowing lawns. It seems that having a lawn mowing business is the gateway for many budding entrepreneurs. I started mowing lawns solo, but soon had enough business to convince my brothers and friends to join me. I fixed up a few clunky lawn mowers, and we were officially off to the races. It didn't take long to realize that without instructions, I had total mayhem on my hands—confused and frustrated customers, not to mention my lawn mowing equipment getting thrashed and broken. That's when I realized that consistency is equally, if not more, important than quality. I had to teach my lawn mowing team the processes that had made me successful in the first place. Here are the steps I took each and every time one of us mowed a customer's lawn:

1.  Present yourself well. I would tuck in my shirt and wipe the sweat and dirt off my hands and face before knocking on the customer's door with a big smile on my face and saying, "Hello, I am here to mow your lawn today. It will take me about an hour and a half. Is now an okay time?"

2.  Clear the lawn. Before mowing a lawn, I looked it over carefully and removed all the balls and junk. I picked up any dog mess, trash, or anything else that was on the lawn.

3.  Trim the lawn. I used the trimmer to trim around the entire edge of the lawn before I began mowing.

4.  Check the oil in the lawn mower.

5.  Check the gas in the lawn mower and make sure the tank is full. I only put gas in the lawn mower while it was on the sidewalk so that I didn't kill any grass if I spilled.

6. I went to the center of the lawn and picked a point straight across the lawn. Then I shot for a straight line. Everyone likes nice straight lines better than random tire marks across their lawns.

7. I followed the wheel patterns through the entire lawn to keep all of the lines straight. If the lines got off, I corrected them.

8. I emptied the grass bag before it got full so that clumps of grass would not spill out on the lawn.

9. After mowing, I cleaned up the lawn and yard. I raked any grass or debris that was left on the lawn and blew or swept the sidewalks off. Everyone likes their yard to look neat and clean after the grass is mowed.

10. I respectfully invoiced the customer. I wiped the sweat off my face and the dirt off my hands and knocked on the customer's door. I then handed them the invoice for mowing the lawn and put a piece of candy or a package of seeds with it as I thanked them for the opportunity of mowing their lawn.

This process example may seem rather elementary, but I had to mow a lot of lawns before I learned that it took a lot less time and the lawn looked much neater if I trimmed the edges before I mowed. I also learned that when I was having other people mow lawns for me, they all wanted to do it their own way. But I knew that my customers had hired me to mow their lawns because they knew they would have straight lines and they would like the way their lawn looked after it was mowed. They also loved that I gave them a packet of seeds or a piece of candy as my signature when I finished. So, I had to document the processes and teach these things to my employees so they would know what my customers expected.

My wife worked for Kentucky Fried Chicken while she was a teenager. They have a list posted to the wall above the biscuit machine detailing the exact steps for making their delicious, fluffy biscuits as well as other lists detailing each step in making their chicken and every other menu item. This keeps the consistency and quality that is expected each time a customer goes to eat at any KFC.

I used to love to eat at a regional fast-food restaurant that sells delicious chicken and rice bowls. But one time when I went there, the dish I was served did not taste the same. I commented to the person at the counter, "Something tastes really weird in my chicken." He said, "Oh, yeah, our normal supplier was out of the chicken we normally use, so we had to use different chicken today." I thought this was just a fluke, so I went back the following week. This time the chicken tasted much spicier than usual, and it was even worse than the previous week. I mentioned it to the guy at the front again and he said, "Yes, we had to try an even different supplier this week." I went back a few more times, but each time the chicken was different. Not surprisingly, this franchise went out of business not long after. Whatever the size or complexity of your business, processes matter!

In zag number 2, you have to document the processes that

led to your initial success. You need to put these into bite-sized processes that other people can follow. That is why I instructed my employees to trim the grass before they mowed the lawn and put the gas into the mower while it was on cement so as to not kill the grass. I had made all these mistakes and had learned from them, so I institutionalized what I had learned.

As you document your processes, remember to learn from the mistakes you made driving to profitability. Documenting what not to do is as important as documenting what to do. You want to have something in place that makes people think twice about making the same mistakes, and it will help if you have already proven what doesn't work.

And we are fortunate to be living right now as AI can dramatically help create your Standard Operating Procedures. You can leverage AI to streamline and optimize these processes, making them more efficient and easier to follow.

## THE FIVE-MINUTE WHITEBOARD

It is vital in our businesses to establish cadences of accountability. I have seen many models used through the years, but by far my favorite is the one that I developed called the Five-Minute Whiteboard. This is incredibly powerful for both in-person businesses and online businesses. I have found that it works very effectively with up to about fifteen employees. This is designed to ensure that everyone on the team knows which of our tasks are the 20 percent that will result in 80 percent of the results.

I've installed a huge whiteboard in our office. We write each team member's name across the top with a different color of marker. In our staff meetings, each person then brain dumps everything they have to do during the coming week. It doesn't matter whether it is a small little thing or a really big thing—we list everything. After everyone has listed their tasks, they then put an "A" "B" or "C" next to each task to give it a priority ("A" for vital, "C" not so much).

We then all stand back and look over the board. We're able to see that if this person doesn't get something done, this other person won't be able to get her highest priority done. We also discuss if items need a higher priority or if they are not really that important.

As the week goes on, each team member crosses off completed tasks. They also have the ability to write on someone else's list. If there is a task anywhere on the board that is critical to you, you can increase its priority. I have even put big red circles around someone's task, letting them know that it is getting to be a hot potato in the business and that they need to deal with it. When one team member's list is getting shorter, they're expected to help someone else with their list and cross off items.

I now have remote teams and individuals engaged with me all over the world. We have adapted the concept of the whiteboard to an online Google Sheet deploying the same concepts. This serves the same purpose as the physical whiteboard and allows us all, in different locations, to see the priorities, what everyone is working on, and have the same outcome.

There are three very powerful functions that this Five-Minute Whiteboard fills:

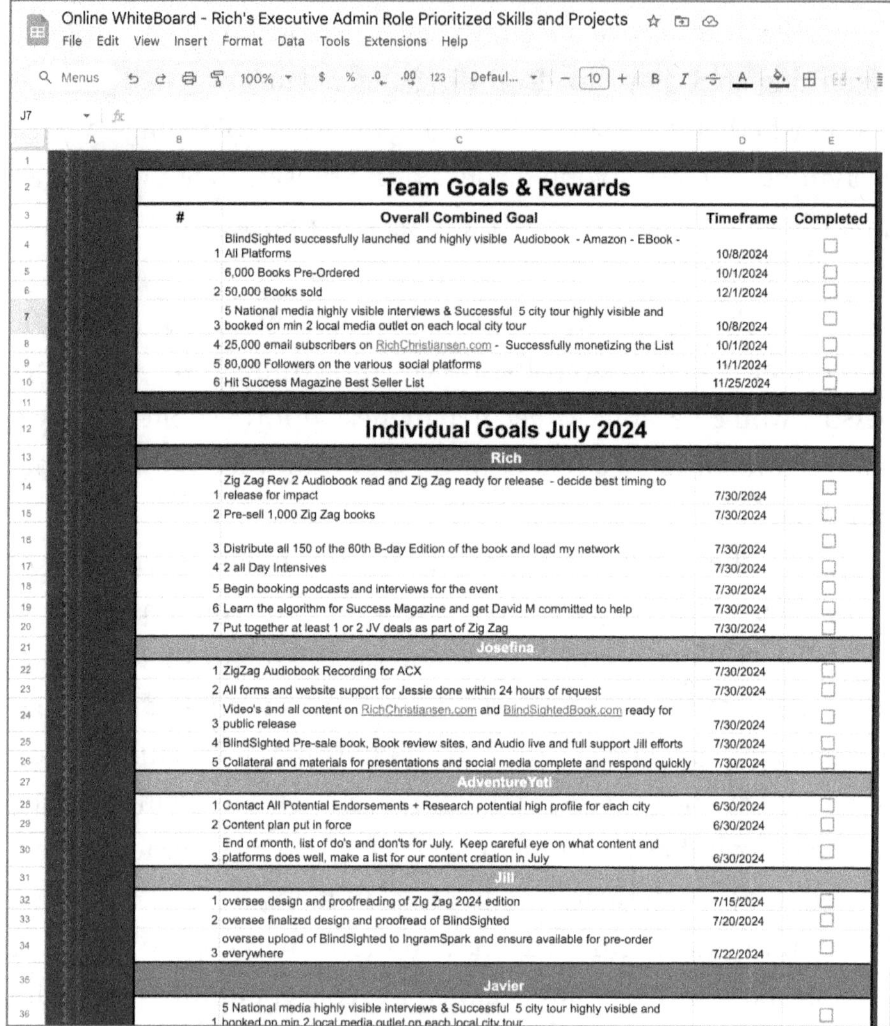

Online WhiteBoard - Rich's Executive Admin Role Prioritized Skills and Projects

**Team Goals & Rewards**

| # | Overall Combined Goal | Timeframe | Completed |
|---|---|---|---|
| 1 | BlindSighted successfully launched and highly visible Audiobook - Amazon - EBook - All Platforms | 10/8/2024 | ☐ |
|  | 6,000 Books Pre-Ordered | 10/1/2024 | ☐ |
| 2 | 50,000 Books sold | 12/1/2024 | ☐ |
| 3 | 5 National media highly visible interviews & Successful 5 city tour highly visible and booked on min 2 local media outlet on each local city tour | 10/8/2024 | ☐ |
| 4 | 25,000 email subscribers on RichChristiansen.com - Successfully monetizing the List | 10/1/2024 | ☐ |
| 5 | 80,000 Followers on the various social platforms | 11/1/2024 | ☐ |
| 6 | Hit Success Magazine Best Seller List | 11/25/2024 | ☐ |

**Individual Goals July 2024**

| # | Rich | Timeframe | Completed |
|---|---|---|---|
| 1 | Zig Zag Rev 2 Audiobook read and Zig Zag ready for release - decide best timing to release for impact | 7/30/2024 | ☐ |
| 2 | Pre-sell 1,000 Zig Zag books | 7/30/2024 | ☐ |
| 3 | Distribute all 150 of the 60th B-day Edition of the book and load my network | 7/30/2024 | ☐ |
| 4 | 2 all Day Intensives | 7/30/2024 | ☐ |
| 5 | Begin booking podcasts and interviews for the event | 7/30/2024 | ☐ |
| 6 | Learn the algorithm for Success Magazine and get David M committed to help | 7/30/2024 | ☐ |
| 7 | Put together at least 1 or 2 JV deals as part of Zig Zag | 7/30/2024 | ☐ |

| # | Josefina | Timeframe | Completed |
|---|---|---|---|
| 1 | ZigZag Audiobook Recording for ACX | 7/30/2024 | ☐ |
| 2 | All forms and website support for Jessie done within 24 hours of request | 7/30/2024 | ☐ |
| 3 | Video's and all content on RichChristiansen.com and BlindSightedBook.com ready for public release | 7/30/2024 | ☐ |
| 4 | BlindSighted Pre-sale book, Book review sites, and Audio live and full support Jill efforts | 7/30/2024 | ☐ |
| 5 | Collateral and materials for presentations and social media complete and respond quickly | 7/30/2024 | ☐ |

| # | AdventureYeti | Timeframe | Completed |
|---|---|---|---|
| 1 | Contact All Potential Endorsements + Research potential high profile for each city | 6/30/2024 | ☐ |
| 2 | Content plan put in force | 6/30/2024 | ☐ |
| 3 | End of month, list of do's and dont's for July. Keep careful eye on what content and platforms does well, make a list for our content creation in July | 6/30/2024 | ☐ |

| # | Jill | Timeframe | Completed |
|---|---|---|---|
| 1 | oversee design and proofreading of Zig Zag 2024 edition | 7/15/2024 | ☐ |
| 2 | oversee finalized design and proofread of BlindSighted | 7/20/2024 | ☐ |
| 3 | oversee upload of BlindSighted to IngramSpark and ensure available for pre-order everywhere | 7/22/2024 | ☐ |

| # | Javier | Timeframe | Completed |
|---|---|---|---|
| 1 | 5 National media highly visible interviews & Successful 5 city tour highly visible and booked on min 2 local media outlet on each local city tour | | ☐ |

Instantly, everyone on the team knows what the critical tasks are for the week.

The team knows when someone is overburdened, and they can help him or her out. If John has fifteen "A" items on his list, the rest of the team knows not to dump more onto him. If Matt only has a few smaller items, he knows he must help John.

It provides accountability and transparency in the

organization, which ensures that everyone is actually producing and being effective.

I have found that the Five-Minute Whiteboard is the most powerful when we do it on a Friday afternoon rather than the first thing Monday morning. This allows everyone to subconsciously begin thinking through their task lists so that on Monday morning they are geared up and ready to attack.

I remember yet one more example of how effective our Five-Minute Whiteboard is. We had a situation where we had a large shipment that had been stalled due to some shipping infrastructure issues. As a result, we had $150,000 worth of merchandise just sitting in our warehouse waiting to be shipped—and holding up our cash flow. The day finally came when the truck was able to come, but it showed up two-and-a-half hours earlier than scheduled. Loading this truck and getting this shipment off was an "A+" item on our warehouse manager's list. When the truck showed up early, not one word was said. Everyone on the team just got up, put on their coats and gloves, and went out into the cold parking lot to help Cameron load the truck. Everyone knew this shipment was critical to our business and essential to the cash flow. Everyone understood and was in tune with the environment of the company. That is the power of the Five-Minute Whiteboard.

## LEVERAGING AI FOR PROCESSES AND EFFICIENCY

In today's fast-paced business environment, integrating AI resources into your workflow can significantly streamline processes and enhance efficiency. AI tools are not just an added advantage but a necessity for modern businesses looking to scale and optimize their operations. Among the top resources available, ChatGPT stands out as an exceptional tool for generating ideas, drafting documents, automating customer service responses, and much more. Here's how you can effectively leverage AI, including ChatGPT, to transform your business processes.

AI tools can help automate repetitive tasks, analyze large sets of data for actionable insights, and provide predictive analytics to guide decision-making. They can be particularly useful in creating Standard Operating Procedures (SOPs), where consistency and accuracy are paramount. The key is to integrate these tools seamlessly into your existing workflows to maximize their potential.

## HERE ARE 10 AI TOOLS THAT CAN DRAMATICALLY HELP WITH PROCESS AND EFFICIENCY:

I realize that writing this section will necessitate another update in a few years, given the rapid pace of technological advancement. It is hard for us to even fathom what technology and resources will be available in five years. With this in mind, I offer today's perspective on valuable tools.

1. **ChatGPT by OpenAI**: Ideal for drafting documents, automating customer interactions, generating ideas, and providing instant answers to a wide range of queries.

2. **Zapier**: Automates workflows by connecting your apps

and services, enabling them to work together without manual intervention.

3. **Trello**: Uses AI to manage project tasks and workflows, helping teams stay organized and on track.

4. **Monday.com**: An AI-powered work operating system that helps teams manage projects and workflows with customizable templates and automation.

5. **Asana**: Leverages AI to improve project management and collaboration, ensuring tasks are assigned and completed efficiently.

6. **Grammarly**: Uses AI to enhance writing by checking for grammar, punctuation, and style, ensuring all written communication is professional and error-free.

7. **Xero**: An accounting software that uses AI to automate invoicing, payroll, and expense tracking, making financial management more efficient.

8. **HubSpot**: Integrates AI to automate marketing, sales, and customer service processes, improving overall customer relationship management.

9. **Hootsuite**: Uses AI to manage social media accounts, schedule posts, and analyze performance, ensuring a consistent and effective social media presence.

10. **UiPath**: A leading RPA (Robotic Process Automation) tool that automates repetitive tasks across various applications, significantly improving operational efficiency.

## IMPLEMENTING AI IN YOUR WORKFLOW

To start implementing AI in your workflow, identify the repetitive and time-consuming tasks that could benefit from automation. For instance, use ChatGPT to draft your SOPs or customer responses. Tools like Zapier and UiPath can automate data entry and routine processes, freeing up your team to focus on more strategic tasks. Project management tools like Trello and Asana can ensure that your team stays on track and deadlines are met.

By strategically incorporating these AI tools, you not only enhance efficiency but also ensure consistency and accuracy in your operations. This approach will not only relieve pressure from you but will also set a strong foundation for scalable growth and a higher valuation for potential exits. Remember, a well-documented and automated process is a key factor that purchasers of a business look for, as it signifies a stable and scalable operation.

## CHECKLIST: TOP 10 AREAS TO NAIL DOWN PROCESSES IN YOUR NEW BUSINESS

1. **Customer Service**
   - Answering inquiries and handling complaints like a pro

- Smooth onboarding for new customers
- Gathering and acting on feedback

2. **Sales and Marketing**
   - Generating leads and following up like a boss
   - Managing your sales pipeline effectively
   - Planning and executing killer marketing campaigns

3. **Financial Management**
   - Streamlining invoicing and payment collection
   - Keeping a close eye on expenses
   - Budgeting and forecasting to stay ahead of the game

4. **Human Resources**
   - Recruiting and hiring the right people
   - Onboarding and training your team
   - Evaluating performance and keeping everyone motivated

5. **Product/Service Development**
   - Designing and developing your products or services
   - Ensuring top-notch quality through testing
   - Launching and iterating based on feedback

6. **Operations and Logistics**
   - Managing your supply chain like a well-oiled

machine
- Keeping inventory in check
- Ensuring smooth order fulfillment and shipping

7. **IT and Data Management**
   - Regular data backup and recovery plans
   - Implementing strong cybersecurity measures
   - Maintaining software and hardware

8. **Compliance and Legal**
   - Staying on top of industry regulations
   - Managing contracts efficiently
   - Protecting your intellectual property

9. **Project Management**
   - Assigning and tracking tasks
   - Setting milestones and monitoring progress
   - Identifying and mitigating risks

10. **Customer Relationship Management (CRM)**
    - Managing customer data effectively
    - Implementing follow-up and retention strategies
    - Making the most of your CRM software

## HOW TO MAKE THESE PROCESSES WORK FOR YOU

➤ **Document Everything**: Write down each step clearly so

your team can follow along without any hiccups.

> **Assign Responsibility**: Make sure everyone knows who's in charge of what.

> **Leverage AI and Automation**: Tools like ChatGPT can help streamline these processes, saving you time and headaches.

> **Review Regularly**: Keep an eye on your processes and tweak them as needed to keep things running smoothly.

> **Train and Support Your Team**: Make sure your team is up to speed with regular training and support.

By focusing on these key areas and setting up solid processes, you'll free up your time, create consistency, and pave the way for a successful exit down the line. Remember, well-documented processes are what buyers look for—they want to see that your business is a smooth-running machine. So, get those processes in place and watch your business thrive!

## SUMMARY

After you have hit profitability in zig number 1, zag number 2 is all about adding resources. You are making the transition from working harder to working smarter. You are going from determination to discipline. You are going from being the butcher, the baker, and the candlestick maker to cheerleading a team and turning over control to others. Remember that this will involve letting your hires make some mistakes and do things a little differently than you would. But if you do this effectively, you are increasing your profitability, adding resources into the system, and documenting the processes.

This is where the culture of your company will be defined. It's one of the most fun phases of your business, where stories will come that will define the life of your business—good and bad! Your values will be tested for the first time, so hold strong.

CHAPTER 6

# ZIG NUMBER 3—ADDING SCALE

Of all the chapters, this one has always felt the least tactical. Yet, over the years, I've realized that this stage is the most elusive and often takes multiple attempts. It's the most complex, often more art than science. In this revision, I have added a bit more practical guidance.

The third zig is about adding scale to your endeavor. After securing cash flow and integrating resources and processes, you need to scale your product or service to reach the masses. Simply put, scale means something that can be replicated or sold repeatedly.

Take the music industry, for example. There are incredibly talented studio musicians who get hired to play for top recording artists. They come into the studio, lay down their tracks, get paid handsomely, and move on to their next gig. While they live comfortably, their paycheck is a one-time deal. On the other hand, the artist who writes and records the song gets royalties every time the song is downloaded, sold, or played on the radio. By scaling their talents and business strategies, recording artists receive numerous checks and enjoy a great lifestyle.

Business becomes truly enjoyable when you make money while sleeping, vacationing, or working on your next project. I recall the first time this happened to me. I was bedridden for a few weeks, so I brainstormed a small business idea, set up a website, optimized it for search engines, and went to bed. The next morning, I discovered I had made $37.50 while asleep! (That number grew over the following days.) This is the power of scale.

My colleagues and I often say, "Nail it, then scale it." This means that during the first two zigs and zags, you're figuring out how to solidify your business—establishing the discipline, effort, and processes that will make it successful. In zig number 1, you focus on profitability. In zag number 2, you add resources. In zig number 3, you need to develop a model that can be quickly replicated and get your product out to the masses. This is the "scaling it" part.

I've sometimes ruffled feathers by stating, "I never want to be a doctor or a lawyer!" My point isn't to offend professionals like my brother, a successful doctor. My point is that doctors and lawyers must physically or mentally work to make money. I prefer making money beyond the time I'm actively working.

## SCALING FOR SUCCESS

I have a dentist friend who wants to develop a product to simplify filling cavities but feels stuck drilling teeth all day. I've explained that he needs to zigzag. With his existing business's cash flow, he can add resources and scale. By bringing another dentist and more hygienists into his practice, he could free up time to work on his product, create a local testing and promotional channel, and eventually build an online presence.

Another example is a talented chiropractor who scaled his business by compiling his successful practices into a system he sells to other chiropractors. He created a training program that's now widely known, helping others while profiting without direct involvement.

## THE FOUR RULES OF SCALE

I've developed four rules for creating scalable businesses. While I occasionally break these rules, I do so deliberately. These are my guidelines based on my skills and values; you'll need to find what works for you.

1. **Ride a Wave:** Choose businesses on a rising trend. Just like surfers, catching the right wave can propel you forward. Timing is crucial—getting on and off at the

right time matters.

2. **Transactional Businesses:** Position yourself in the middle of a transaction. Credit card companies, for example, earn a percentage of every transaction, benefiting from convenience on both sides.

3. **Own the Customer:** Ensure you have a direct relationship with your customers. Avoid being at the mercy of brokers or middlemen, as this limits your ability to address issues directly.

4. **I Like Digital Assets:** This is a personal preference, but I love digital assets. Retail doesn't suit me—I lack the discipline and patience for it, and it doesn't scale as well for me. Once I build a website or digital application, it can serve an unlimited number of people. A retail store, by contrast, is limited by physical space and location. Digital assets offer far more options and scalability.

## SCALING BEYOND DIGITAL

In 2022, Michael Martinez, the owner of a boutique coffee roastery in Austin, Texas, faced a critical juncture. His business, Austin Brews, had built a strong local reputation, but growth was stagnant, and he was struggling to keep up with rising costs. During a casual conversation with a tech-savvy friend, Michael was introduced to the idea of subscription-based services. Intrigued by the potential for recurring revenue, he decided to pivot his business model.

Michael launched an online subscription service, offering customers monthly deliveries of his freshly roasted coffee beans. He invested in a user-friendly website with a seamless subscription management system. To attract subscribers, he used targeted social media advertising and partnered with local influencers who shared their positive experiences with Austin Brews. He also added personalized touches, such as allowing customers to customize their coffee preferences and including handwritten notes in each delivery.

The subscription service quickly took off. Within a few months, Michael's subscriber base grew significantly, providing a steady and predictable income stream. This newfound financial stability allowed him to scale his operations, invest in better roasting equipment, and hire additional staff. By mid-2023, Austin Brews had expanded its reach beyond Texas, shipping to coffee enthusiasts nationwide. Michael's strategic shift to a subscription model not only revitalized his business but also set it on a path of sustainable growth, illustrating the power of innovation and adaptability in today's market.

## BREAKING DOWN THE CONCEPT

Zig Number 3 requires another shift in mindset. In Zig Number 1, you're working hard on everything. In Zag Number 2, you become the head cheerleader, defining processes. Zig Number 3 is about deliberate planning. It's cerebral and requires stepping back from the minutiae, analyzing, and determining what levers to flip for significant impact.

# 5 PIECES OF ADVICE TO SCALE YOUR BUSINESS QUICKLY

Scaling a business quickly requires strategic planning, effective execution, and the ability to adapt to new challenges. Here are five key pieces of advice to help you achieve rapid growth:

1. **Focus on Customer Experience:**
   Deliver exceptional customer service to build loyalty and encourage word-of-mouth referrals. Personalize interactions, respond promptly to inquiries, and resolve issues efficiently. Happy customers are more likely to become repeat buyers and brand advocates, which is crucial for rapid scaling.

2. **Build a Subscription Model:**
   Develop a subscription service around your products or services. This approach stabilizes income by providing a predictable revenue stream and enhances customer retention. Subscriptions create ongoing engagement with your brand and can lead to higher customer lifetime value. By securing recurring revenue, you can invest more confidently in growth initiatives and scale your business faster.

3. **Build Strategic Partnerships:**
   Form partnerships with other businesses that complement your offerings. This can help you reach new markets and expand your customer base. For example,

if you own a fitness apparel company, partnering with gyms or fitness influencers can provide mutual benefits and open up new growth avenues. Additionally, offer a referral fee and ensure it is paid quickly. This tactic has been highly effective in rapidly acquiring new clients.

4. **Automate and Optimize Processes:**
Streamline your operations by automating repetitive tasks. Use software tools for inventory management, customer relationship management (CRM), and financial tracking. Automation not only saves time but also reduces the likelihood of errors, allowing you to focus on strategic growth activities.

5. **Hire a Young, Hungry Digital Marketing Team:**
Invest in a dynamic and motivated digital marketing team. Young professionals often bring fresh perspectives and innovative ideas to the table. They are adept at navigating social media platforms and can create engaging content that resonates with your target audience. Encourage them to leverage the latest trends and technologies to maximize your online presence. By incentivizing customers to share their experiences and reviews on social media, your brand can rapidly gain visibility and attract a broader audience.

By implementing these strategies, you can position your business for quick and sustainable scaling, ensuring you meet the growing demands of your expanding customer base.

# SUMMARY

Zig Number 3 involves a major shift in mindset. You are no longer working in your business; you are working on your business. This shift requires deliberate planning and a strategic approach, balancing hard work with cerebral effort. Use tools like The Decision Matrix to make informed decisions and keep refining your approach to achieve scalable success.

CHAPTER 7

# GUARDRAILS

As you zigzag down that mountain toward your goal, you need to realize there are hazards on either side of the ski run. Ski resorts groom and prepare the areas intended for skiers; however, experienced skiers know that just beyond the groomed runs are trees, rocks, potential avalanches, cliffs, and other dangers that may cause injury or even death. The same is true in business and life. If we're smart, we establish guardrails to keep us away from perils and on the groomed slopes that lead to our goals. Guardrails are not limiting; rather, they keep us safe and allow us to move with more confidence.

Entrepreneurs are expected to be doggedly determined and at the same time know when it is time to shut things down. By pre-setting the rules of engagement and agreeing to them, you can avoid making foolish emotional decisions that put you, your family, and your future at risk. Guardrails should be an integral part of all that you do, keeping you focused and secure as you navigate your path.

Some people think zigzagging is easy or a lazy person's game. The reality is it requires great discipline and control. Any skier will tell you that traversing a steep mountain requires a strong back and legs, quick reflexes, and agility, while heading straight down is far less taxing. That is, until you crash and burn.

To avoid disaster, you're going to want to create boundaries and set guardrails, which will keep you headed in the direction of your goal—and away from your own personal train wreck or avalanche.

## KEEPING YOUR ZIGZAGS UNDER CONTROL

When you are beginning to head toward your beacon in the fog, you want to concentrate on three zigs and zags at a time. That will keep you focused and under control. To help you with that, think in terms of devoting 65 percent of your time and resources on zig number 1 (driving to profitability), with 25 percent spent on planning and preparing for zag number 2 (adding resources and processes once you get to cash). The final 10 percent of your time and resources should be spent planning how you want to scale your undertaking in zig number 3 (creating scale). If you're looking beyond three zigs, life gets too complex.

Once you have hit zig number 1 and your business is profitable, you need to turn and head toward zag number 2. It's easy, once you have cash coming in, to think you can skip making the turn. But if you just stay in zig number 1, you may miss out on the dreams and goals defined as your true beacon in the fog. (And remember, cash alone is not a beacon worth pursuing.)

Once you are profitable, you should shift and spend about 65 percent of your time and energy on zag number 2, with 25 percent of your time spent on planning and preparing for zig number 3. Again, if you do not make this next turn, you may find yourself with a lot of resources, but never hitting that big goal. The last 10 percent of your time and efforts can then go toward setting another series of zigs that will help you get even closer to your beacon in the fog.

Remember, as you're zigzagging, to look for dangers or pitfalls that are in your way. There have been lots of times when I've been skiing on a run I thought I knew well, only to spot a rock or bare spot that has reared its ugly head. By remaining agile and in control, you can avoid whatever obstacle is lurking.

In the business Curtis and I were working on, we began by setting our goal and then laying out our zigs and zags. Our first two zigs were clear, but our third zag was way off in the distance. As we hit profitability and then began working on adding resources, it became evident that our initial plan did not have as high a probability of success as several other opportunities we had uncovered as we were working through our first two zigs. So, we adjusted.

What you do not want to change, however, is the present

target you are shooting for. Keeping control of your zigs will help you stay focused on that target, rather than turning hither and yon whenever the urge presents itself. In my experience, if you begin thinking beyond three zigs, you will actually lose sight of the path you are on. It will probably take you more than three zigs and zags to get to your final beacon in the fog, but only look out at three at one time. As you complete each goal, take a minute to celebrate, but afterward climb a tree and look out above the fog toward your beacon, making certain you are still on course. Then set another zig that will lead you in the direction you need to go.

A common question I hear is, "If I am making money, why do I want to make the next turn? Wouldn't it be better to just keep making money?" I have seen many examples of people who just kept chasing cash. Often, these are small, family-owned businesses where mom and dad are working day and night. They make enough money to cover their expenses or maybe to live comfortably; but by not adding resources, they never seem to be able to enjoy life away from the shop.

I have a neighbor who owns a candy-making business. He is the only one who knows how to make the candy. His wife works in the front, taking orders and keeping the books. This is a very labor-intensive business that requires this couple to work every day. They've lamented to me on many occasions that they never dare take a day off to go on a vacation or to enjoy their life because they are afraid of what their absence will do to the business. Just think what they could do if they would go to the next zig, document their processes, hire a few employees, and grow their company, even just a little. When people won't make the turn after hitting zig number 1, they get stuck—even though they may have a bunch of cash.

Everyone's situation is different in significant ways; but, as you create your own set of guardrails to control your zigs and zags, here are four elements that I always include in my guardrails:

1.  **A financial number.** How much money are you willing to spend on each zig? If you do not hit your goal within this budget, you are not profitable and may have to check your idea off as a failure. Do not chase losing bets.

2.  **Quantity of time.** How many hours a week are you going to dedicate to the project. I have personally over allocated and underallocated the quantity of time and either starved or burned out projects because of it.

3.  **Duration of time.** How long are you willing to work on this venture before hitting your financial target? Are you going to chase cash for a month, a year, or 10 years?

4.  **Relationship Capital.** The most valuable asset that you have is your relationships. I do not expose every idea and every business to all my relationships. What relationships are you willing to expose to your new venture?

## BUILDING YOUR GUARDRAILS

The guardrails you create must be closely aligned with the values you set in Chapter 3. You need to have people in your life who will tell you when you are out of bounds. I have a good friend who was a successful and well-known college basketball coach until he got embroiled in some politics and lost his job. We were talking, not long after that, and he shared what I consider to be a very profound insight. He said, "Rich, when I was winning championships, everyone laughed at my jokes. Now they only laugh when my jokes are actually funny." You need someone in your inner circle who knows you and whom you trust to tell you if your jokes are funny or not.

Alex Mendozian is a teleseminar trainer. We had discussed the possibility of working on a project together. Before we began, he called me and said, "Rich, I have some good news and some bad news. I'd really like to work with you. That is the good news. The bad news is, before I do, I need to have an intervention in your life." I pushed back, thinking, *What is he talking about? I don't have a drinking or a drug problem!* He continued, "Yes, you need an intervention!" He then got my wife and his executive assistant on the phone and explained he was having this intervention because I had to quit saying "Yes" to everyone and everything. Warren Buffett once said, "The difference between successful people and very successful people is that very successful people say 'no' to almost everything" (Maddock, G. Michael & Viton, Raphael Louis, "The Stop-Doing List," *Bloomberg Businessweek*, December 7, 2010).

Sometimes, in your zeal to reach your beacon in the fog, everything seems possible. It's a time when you're generating a lot of ideas. It's a time when, out of necessity, you need to fire, fire, fire, and then aim. I refer to this part of zig number 1 as the time I have to weave gold out of straw. During this time, I may not have a lot of resources, and I may find myself holding things together with duct tape and bailing wire. As I'm trying to get something to work that will generate cash, I find myself saying, "Yes, yes, yes, no; … yes, yes, yes, maybe."

Once I get to the next zag, I have to create systematic and organized processes so I can hire employees and teach them how to make the business work. During this time, I find myself saying "No" about half the time. Part of that involves learning the discipline of delegating and letting others do the work for me.

Getting to the third zig demonstrates that I have achieved success by reaching cash, creating an organization that is working. Now I need to scale it. This is a much more controlled phase of the process because I do not want to destroy what I have just created. I finally have all of the gears meshing, and I now need to figure out how to scale the business so it will generate income independent of my direct involvement. During this period, I find myself needing to say "No" far more often.

Another guardrail you need to put in place is identifying and empowering those people in your life who will help you say "No" and who will let you know when you are heading out of bounds. For me, those people include my wife and my executive assistant, both of whom are excellent at letting me know when I am crossing the lines I've established. My children will sometimes even tell me when I am out of line—and I've learned to listen. My business partner is another person I make sure I listen to. Unfortunately, it's rare that your subordinates will point out when you're heading toward danger. Some see things quite clearly, but many either are making sure they look good in your eyes or are afraid of your reaction. If one speaks up, listen, unless it feels like they're stroking your ego.

# STAYING OUT OF THE WEEDS

Weeds are diversions, inefficiencies, and even short-term successes that distract you from the course you have set for yourself. Weeds can be either negative or positive forces. They may take the form of being stuck with a large team that you just can't find a way to keep motivated. They might involve becoming so mesmerized with the profitability you've achieved that you forget to move on to your next step. Your personal weeds might have to do with a tendency to continually react to everyone else's demands instead of moving toward your goal.

Just as important as establishing the values that will serve as your road map is your need to set up the guardrails that will keep you out of the weeds. The guardrails you'll need to keep you out of the weeds are very personal and will differ according to your circumstances and objectives. Everyone should have guardrails in place for the various parts of each zig and zag so that you are always in control of your financial number, your allocation of time, your duration of time, and your financial target. Your other guardrails will be determined by factors such as your tolerance for risk, your family's tolerance for risk, your value system, and what portion of your personal network you are willing to expose to your endeavor.

I'm going to share some of my guardrails, but remember that these are my rules, not yours. I share them only to illustrate how important it is to give careful, specific thought to your guardrails, rather than attempting to put them in place when you're in the middle of heading over the cliff. Here are some of my guardrails:

➤ I will not jeopardize the financial stability of my home or family. I am not going to mortgage my house for my business.

➤ I like to keep my teams small (under fifteen people).

➤ I will be very careful in taking venture capital. I want to retain ownership in my companies.

➤ I must control the finances of my business.

➤ I will not sign personal guarantees on a business I do not personally control.

➤ I will protect my personal network.

➤ I will not get involved in a business that goes against my personal moral values.

➤ I will not do anything illegal or unethical.

➤ I will not work with people I do not enjoy. Whether it is a customer, a vendor, or an employee, life is too short to work with miserable people or with people who make me miserable.

My list is actually longer, but these are a few examples of my guardrails. If I find myself getting near the edge on any of these, my wife, my business partner, and my executive admin each knows me well enough to tell me I am starting to cross the line. And I expect them not to stand by silently.

<table>
<tr><td>Out-of-Bounds Worksheet</td></tr>
<tr><td>List the people that you trust to tell you when you are out-of-bounds. This is your "out of bounds" network.</td></tr>
<tr><td>List the guardrails that will keep you from going out-of-bounds.</td></tr>
<tr><td>List 4 or 5 ways you will know when you are heading out-of-bounds. Is it a gut feeling, panic, scarcity mindset, or something else?</td></tr>
<tr><td>Refer back to the resource list in Chapter 4 to determine exactly where you need to change direction on each zig and zag. List those direction changes.</td></tr>
<tr><td>Have a direct conversation with each member of your out-of-bounds network. Make sure they clearly understand what your guardrails are and what their responsibility is to keep you within those bounds.</td></tr>
</table>

## SUMMARY

As you are traveling toward your beacon in the fog, you will need guardrails to keep you from heading over a cliff or wandering into the weeds. For each of your zigs, you should establish a financial number, an allocation of time, a duration of time, and the relationships you expose for that particular zig. You then need to create a list of the other guardrails that will keep you out of the weeds. Finally, remember the need to establish a network of trusted associates who will keep you from heading out of bounds or drifting toward the edge of a cliff. These guardrails will grow out of and be aligned with the values you defined in Chapter 3. They will then have the power to keep you on target as you zigzag toward your beacon in the fog.

CHAPTER 8

# REWARDS—PLANTING HIDDEN TREASURES

Planting hidden treasures is the most fun of all the concepts in Zig Zag. It is also how you can keep yourself motivated as well as your team focused on what really matters. Seventy-percent of the early entrepreneurship game is psychology, and this is my secret weapon. This works, this is fun, and I promise you that if you do this, you will see incredible results with your team.

As you have been rushing from goal to goal or from zig

to zag, have you ever found yourself asking, "Why am I doing this?" If you haven't created and implemented a system of rewards for yourself and those around you, you're going to find yourself burning out long before you reach your beacon in the fog. Success and money alone are insufficient motivators. I have found that if I tie a reward to the successful completion of each zig, I stay far more motivated than if I never pause to enjoy some benefit specifically tied to its completion. And I find I'm much more enthused about beginning the next zag.

We humans are really not much different from Pavlov's salivating dogs. If we catch a glimpse of a slab of meat (real or proverbial), we will drool, salivate, and do just about anything to get to it. My family had what I had a miserable little dog that was half poodle and half Chihuahua. She was the most high-maintenance little mutt I had ever met. She did not like me, and I did not like her. The problem was the rest of my family loved this dog, so she and I had to put up with each other.

She would have absolutely nothing to do with me, unless I had a little piece of meat in my hand. Then she viewed me as her best friend, and her behavior shifted dramatically. She panted and begged and pleaded for that little piece of meat. And, more importantly, she would do anything I asked. Interestingly, she did not like just any kind of meat. She liked the little slices of cheap lunchmeat that I am sure were not healthy for dogs. Our other dog would eat anything I gave her, but not this little mutt. From the day we got her, I had to find the things that specifically worked for her.

We all have things that motivate us. The legendary football coach Vince Lombardi is attributed with saying, "Coaches who can outline plays on a blackboard are a dime a dozen. The ones who win get inside their player and motivate."

Recognizing that reality, and then consciously and deliberately motivating yourself and your teams using rewards, is one of the most powerful tools I have found, whether it's in my personal, family, or professional life.

When planning and executing each zig and zag, you should attach a reward to each target. If you find the right rewards for your people, once they hit their goal, they will be willing and even anxious to turn toward the next goal.

Every great leader knows how to motivate people. It does not matter if you are a CEO, a coach, a schoolteacher, a middle manager, or a parent: a big part of your job is being the psychologist or therapist who knows how to put out little rewards that get the people around you to behave consistently in working toward the goals you've established. Lee Iacocca said, "Start with good people, lay out the rules, communicate with your employees, motivate them, and reward them. If you do all of those things effectively, you can't miss" (Lee Iacocca, U.S. Businessman, *Talking Straight*, Chapter 4, "Good Business—More in Management," 1988).

## WHAT WILL MOTIVATE YOUR PEOPLE?

Before developing your system of rewards, remember that what motivates one person may not motivate the next. When I was general manager of About.com's web services division, I had working for me a highly talented engineer named Earl. He was, without question, one of our brightest engineers, but I continually struggled to figure out how to motivate this guy. I regularly gave out bonuses, rewards, and incentives that everyone else loved but Earl did not seem to care about. Nothing I offered seemed to motivate him, and I knew his contributions were affected by his apathy toward my rewards system.

As we were planning our first Christmas party, I finally figured out what motivated Earl. During a planning session, he asked if he could play a piano number for the entertainment. I didn't think much about it, but told him that would be fine. The night of the Christmas party, Earl walked in, all decked out in a tuxedo, complete with flowing tails. When he sat down to play the piano, it was clear he cared deeply about his performance, and he delivered his delightful number with the flair of a concert pianist. Everyone cheered and clapped for him, and then he stood up and gave an overly exaggerated bow. From that point forward, I knew what motivated him. He didn't care about things or money. He loved recognition and any opportunity to perform and take a bow.

As the New Year began, I implemented what I dubbed "Lunch and Learn with Earl." Twice each month, we'd have a Lunch and Learn where the company would buy lunch and the junior engineers could visit with this master engineer. They would ask him questions, he would impart his wisdom, and at the end they would all clap and Earl would beam. The junior engineers learned a great deal from Earl, and Earl loved the recognition. Productivity went through the roof.

I had another employee who would always get really excited about the rewards I proposed, but before she achieved her goal, she would simply go out and buy the same thing she was going to be rewarded with. And while she did good work, I knew she could be doing far more. This pattern caused me immense frustration, but I finally found out that what she really wanted was for us to pay for her tuition at school and call it a scholarship. By listening carefully to things she said, I learned that her parents had plenty of money, but they had always drilled into their children how they had gone through college on scholarships. This young woman had good grades, but because she had no real financial need, she hadn't been able to get a scholarship. So, I developed a reward system that provided her with the scholarship she so desperately wanted.

It's also important to figure out what the people you are trying to motivate do not want. I've learned that a reward for one person may actually feel like a punishment for another. A number of years ago we established a reward for the young men who were working for us. We decided to go to Las Vegas and see the Blue Man Group. We set up a very specific goal and also very specific rewards, which included riding on a roller coaster set atop one of the tallest hotels that juts out over the city. These boys, with one exception, worked extra hard because they loved the idea of this trip. When they weren't focused on the work, it was all they talked about. The exception happened to be a different personality type. He was one of our key engineers who was a little shy and did not like big crowds. In fact, the thought of going to Las Vegas with a bunch of loud teenagers couldn't have been less motivating.

Gratefully, he came to me and let me know that he really did not want to go on this trip. So, I found something else that motivated this engineer and took the other boys when they reached their goal. If I had ignored his needs, the outcome might have been tragic. He was a key member of the team, and he could have subconsciously tried to sabotage the goal for the rest of the group because he did not want to go on the trip.

# KEEP YOUR SYSTEM SIMPLE

It's important not to overcomplicate your system of goals and rewards. In one of my early ventures, I created a chart that had eighteen different targets to hit and a simple "REWARD" written across the top. My employees were unclear as to what the priorities were and what the reward would be. Since then, I have found it's best to have three or four target goals to hit, with a very specific reward at the end. The goals we typically fail to achieve are the ones that are complex and unclear.

Employees should also feel free to devise their own systems (within reason, of course). My son and his friends came up with their own motivating reward. They had a Burger King crown they kept in the office. They were all highly competitive, and they would have contests to see which one could create the most web links on a given day. The winner then got to wear the crown. The reward didn't cost me anything, and it was fun to see these 17-year-old boys engage in an all-out push to optimize their websites just for the reward of wearing a paper crown.

One of the benefits of having a team set its own goals and rewards is that the members learn to govern their own behavior. That way I don't have to micromanage my teams.

# AVOID THE ENTITLEMENT MENTALITY

When I was managing Mitsubishi Electric, I was still young and not completely financially stable personally. I had an awesome killer team that was also young and hungry. I began the practice of taking them out to lunch every Friday. I would pay for their lunch myself because I didn't feel the company should have that expense. This was my personal way of showing my appreciation. A few months into this, I ended up in a tough stretch where I was traveling almost nonstop. As a result, there were a few Fridays where we didn't make it to lunch. Soon, there was muttering and complaining. Morale dropped. These employees had become so accustomed to going to lunch each Friday that they felt they were entitled to this perk. What started as a good intention led to my being the bad guy because I did not consistently provide them with their expected lunch.

I had a similar experience with my crew of teenagers. I would stock the fridge with food and soda pops so they could grab something to eat after they finished school and before they started to work. A few times we got so busy I failed to replenish the quickly consumed food items. Almost immediately, some of the boys started murmuring, "I can't believe it, there aren't any burritos or Hot Pockets in the fridge." If I have erred, it is because sometimes I have rewarded too quickly or too often.

## ALLOW FOR SOME FLEXIBILITY

Situations change, and sometimes you need to change with them. I've lived through shifts in markets where even though my team gave an incredible effort, they fell a bit short of the original goal. In those situations, I still gave the reward so the team didn't lose steam. However, be careful not to reward when the reward is not merited.

In a software development company, a team of remote engineers was working on a challenging project with tight deadlines. To motivate the team, the project manager promised a bonus and a paid weekend getaway for everyone if they could consistently deliver a minimum of 10 features per week for a month. The engineers were highly motivated and worked diligently to meet the target.

During the first week, the team delivered 8 features, the second week 11 features, the third week 9 features, and the final week 13 features. Although they didn't achieve the minimum of 10 features every single week, their average delivery was above the target.

Recognizing their overall effort and the quality of work, the project manager decided to reward the team. They received the promised bonus and enjoyed a relaxing weekend getaway. This experience not only boosted their morale but also reinforced the importance of recognizing and rewarding consistent effort, even when specific targets are not perfectly met every single time.

## AMAZING EXAMPLE FROM AN ONLINE COMPANY

I have two sons who work for an amazing, world-class software company called Limble. It is a one hundred percent remote workplace, yet it has created one of the most committed and engaged cultures I have ever seen. People from all over the world are part of this incredible team. This company may be the best example of culture and motivation that I know.

At Limble, they have developed a unique and effective system to foster a positive and collaborative work environment. Each team member is given what they call "tacos." These tacos are a form of recognition currency that employees can give away to their colleagues who are doing good work. With these tacos, employees can purchase items from the company store, all branded with the Limble logo.

This system of giving and receiving tacos creates a culture of goodwill and mutual appreciation. Team members are constantly on the lookout for the good work of their peers, eager to acknowledge and reward it. As a result, employees are motivated to work hard and be recognized by their peers. All this effort and cooperation are driven by the desire to earn tacos and use them to buy company-branded merchandise like mugs, t-shirts, and backpacks.

While most companies struggle to give their swag away, at Limble, the branded items are cherished. My sons wear them around with pride, as if they are wearing Super Bowl rings. The owner of Limble has masterfully figured out how to plant hidden treasures and reward behavior much like Pavlov's salivating dogs. This system not only motivates the employees but also strengthens the sense of belonging and pride in the company, making Limble a shining example of how to build an engaged and dedicated remote workforce.

## THE WHIP

Let's talk for a moment about the opposite of a reward system. I've had partners who used the whip. There certainly are times when you have to discipline. However, my contention is that the whip needs to be used very sparingly—and never as an immediate reaction. If you whip someone (verbally, of course), you may get a burst of incredible performance. But you will inevitably lose your long-term productivity (and your top performers) if you punish too often.

I have seen people who use the whip over and over. Soon the people around them reach the breaking point and basically say, "I don't care. Whip me to death. I am done." They check out, and apathy sets in. I know a young, up-and-coming executive who was a master with the whip. Unfortunately, he was so hungry to prove himself that he burned through all the people around him. Now, no one in our area will work for him.

There is a fine balance between knowing when to reward and knowing when to discipline. When there is an out-of-bounds problem, discipline needs to be meted out. In our home, we do not have the long lists of rules I have seen some parents enforce. Instead, the rules we do have are rules that fit with our core values, and we are very strict with these few rules. I often say to my kids. "You will make some mistakes. That is how you learn. Just don't make the big mistakes!" Too many little rules can create confusion and can actually undermine the more important rules.

## SEEING THE VALUE IN FAILURE

In my prior companies, we would created four sets of quarterly goals for the year. Honestly, I hoped we'd missed one of these goals. I did not want to miss the first set or the second, but if we missed the third set of goals, it would give me an opportunity to point out that this was what a little failure felt like and your success was not guaranteed. I've managed teams that developed a bit too much ego. This can lead to arrogance and long term missed goals. If you handle such situations well, it will bring your team back to where they're hungry and want to win again.

# DON'T GIVE OUT REWARDS UNTIL THEY ARE ACTUALLY EARNED

Being a fundamentally nice guy, I have made the mistake multiple times of giving a reward when the performance didn't warrant it. Every time that I have done this, I have ended up regretting it. Even though you may feel for a minute that you've done the right thing, you've likely created a pattern and behavior system that will bite you in the end. In some cases, being "nice" has been the death knell of my businesses.

My family and I have traveled to Nepal several times, and I am always overwhelmed by the rampant poverty. Like anyone who has traveled there, I have been approached countless times by small children who must beg in the streets for what little they have, and I always ponder what I—as one person with limited means—can do to help.

The last time we were there, several young beggars followed my sons, our two Sherpas, and me everywhere we went. They were filthy, and their ragged clothes were soaked with urine. They approached us repeatedly, gesturing to their mouths and then their stomachs to show us they were hungry. I believe that giving a person a handout does little to change his or her circumstances, but it broke my heart to see these small boys, who were about the ages of my younger boys. Then I hit upon an idea.

We were in the middle of a central square where countless people gather each day to worship and shop. While there are numerous trash cans in the square, no one seems to use them, and the area is covered with what looks like years of debris. I decided I could solve two problems at once, so I offered one of the beggars 100 rupees (about $1.40) for every bag of trash he picked up and put in a trash can. Given that the daily income for an adult in Nepal is about $2, that seemed like a powerful incentive.

What I was asking would have taken a couple of minutes, but this little boy looked at me like I was nuts and ran off. Another little boy approached me, and I made the same offer. He indicated he would do it, but wanted payment up front. Now, I may be a soft touch, but I'm not stupid, so I told him he would get paid upon completion of the work. He, too, ran off.

The third boy who approached me was the dirtiest and scrawniest of the bunch. I really thought my plan had merit, so I upped the offer to 500 rupees. His initial reaction was to give me a look that said, "No one picks up trash. Not even beggars. What kind of crazy American are you?" But this time, I grabbed a bag and started picking up trash myself. He soon joined in and was stuffing trash into his bag as quickly as he could. There was so much trash that our efforts were like trying to drain a pond using a teaspoon, but we were at least doing something to make a dent. And soon others were joining in, including a gentleman who runs a humanitarian organization who saw my impetuous project as having some potential.

When we finished working and I paid the boy, he couldn't have been prouder. And several shopkeepers around the square began making similar offers to other boys who clearly were in need.

I realize that we made a very small dent in the problems of world hunger and cleaning up the environment that day. But I also know that those who watched, including my sons, learned that rewards need to be based on our efforts, not our wishes—and that the right reward system can provide the motivation to get to work and make a difference.

## REWARD YOURSELF

Some people are good about rewarding team members and employees, but they're not so good at rewarding themselves. I've fallen into that trap myself more than once; but I think I've finally learned that if I have an emotional meltdown, it's usually because I haven't followed through on feeding my inner self.

Just as I was taking the frightening leap from being employed at a full-time job to being a full-time entrepreneur, I was playing basketball and blew out my Achilles tendon, which had to be repaired surgically. Six weeks later, while pushing too hard at my physical therapy, I blew it out again. This was a tough time. It's not in my nature to sit around, but all I could do was sit in my bed and work on my computer. I had started a small business, but there was very little I could do to move it forward. I knew that I had the choice to either sink or swim, but I felt myself sinking—and fast.

I finally called my partners into my bedroom, where we talked about our predicament. In mapping out what we could do to salvage the situation, I proposed that if we achieved the success we had our sights on, we would reward ourselves, together with our wives, by going on a cruise. We went to work, and as I lay in bed day after day, I pictured success as sitting with my partners and our wives on an upper deck, toasting our success as we watched the sun set. That image drove me to achieve my goals, even though the odds were stacked against me.

We did indeed hit our goal, and I cannot convey the depth of my joy and satisfaction as we sat around that table and I offered this simple toast, "We did it. We made it."

With that lesson in mind, consider what would have happened had we not taken the celebratory trip? All too often, people intend to give themselves rewards, but then they become martyrs. They start thinking, "I am just too busy," or "I should put this money back into the business." I know that had I not taken that dreamed-about cruise, my subconscious would have revolted, which would have damaged my desire to dig deep and sacrifice in the future.

I use little rewards throughout the day to motivate myself, particularly when I'm really having a tough day. When I'm dealing with difficult issues, I might tell myself something like, "When I get through this, I'm going to go outside and smell the air, and I'm going to watch the ducks for ten minutes." There are all kinds of ways we can reward ourselves quietly throughout the day, and they can help us be more productive and keep our head above water.

## WEEKLY WHITEBOARD MEETINGS

In your weekly whiteboard meetings, it's crucial to always highlight where you are at towards your goal and tell stories that allow your team to salivate on what it will be like as you get your reward. This practice keeps everyone motivated and focused, reinforcing the connection between their hard work and the rewards they will enjoy.

# REWARD SYSTEMS FOR YOUR TEAM WORKSHEET

1. **What common interests do your team have?** List any hobbies, activities, or interests that multiple team members share. How can these interests be incorporated into your reward system?

2. **Who are the strong influencers on your team that can get excited and be your evangelists?** Identify the key team members who are naturally influential and enthusiastic. How can you leverage their influence to promote and sustain the reward system?

3. **What motivates the significant others of your team members?** Consider the interests and preferences of your team members' significant others. How can you design rewards that take these motivations into account?

4. **What demotivates your team?** List factors or situations that decrease motivation and morale among your team members. How can you avoid these demotivators when designing your reward system?

5. **What motivates you?** Reflect on your personal motivators. How can you ensure that the reward system aligns with your own motivations and leadership style?

6. **What about your significant other?** Consider what

motivates your significant other. How can their preferences be considered in the design of the reward system to ensure work-life balance and support?

7. **How could you create cadences of accountability to highlight these rewards?** Outline a plan for regular check-ins, meetings, or updates that will highlight progress towards rewards and keep the team accountable. What methods will you use to track and communicate achievements and rewards?

Use this worksheet to gather insights and tailor your reward system to the unique dynamics of your team, ensuring that it is both motivating and effective.

## SUMMARY

When you are planning out rewards, you need to very specifically tie each reward to the zig or the zag you are heading toward. I always establish time frames, often in the form of quarterly goals. When we make our quarterly goals, we sit down as a team and decide what we want to accomplish. Once we have established the goal, we spend almost as much time discussing what reward we will get when we achieve the goal. Then we make signs and post them all over the office, with the goal written out overtop a picture of the reward.

One of the signs I used in our office had a picture of people snowmobiling. We titled it, "Plowing Our Way to Victory." Around the picture were listed the goals of getting three new clients and having a financial target of monthly recurring profit. Another goal was to hire one more engineer and to retain another engineering client.

For the business my son and his friends worked on, they helped me develop a very specific reward for hitting certain targets. They then posted pictures of the cruise ship we would all board if they met their goals and also the ports we would visit. Sure enough, each of them achieved the goals, and we went for a one-week cruise.

As you set long-term goals, don't overlook the need to reward yourself and your team along the way. These in-between rewards are ones I like to keep random. Then, when I see a team member doing a particularly good job at something, I will hand that member a pair of movie tickets or a gift card. The other day, we sent one of our contract employees a special "thank you" that he was not expecting. Ever since then, he has gone over and above on the work that he does for us because that little reward meant so much to him. Sometimes, random rewards will actually mean more than guaranteeing a treat when you push the same button over and over.

The work you're doing is challenging and difficult, and as you hit each zig, you need to take a break from the intensity.

CHAPTER 9

# AVOIDING THE ALL OR NOTHING TRAP

Of all the chapters in *The Zig Zag Principle*, this is the one that I would like to double down on. This is the real juice in the squeeze, this is where real happiness is found. As a more seasoned entrepreneur who is associated with highly successful individuals in terms of the world, the one and only key factor that really matters is family, trust relationships, and internal peace. My new addition is health and I mean more than just your body; I'm talking about your emotional, spiritual, and mental health.

I grew up in a rural community. My father was completely blind. I am the oldest of four sons, and as long as I can remember, I have had entrepreneurial desires. Despite some lofty ambitions, I was never any kind of stand-out kid. I was one of those boys who was often overlooked, and I spent a lot of time wishing I would not have to take up permanent residence being stuffed in a garbage can. Nonetheless, I had this incredible and deep desire to do something of significance with my life. Whoever figured nerds and entrepreneurs would be the new rock stars?

I remember when I was eighteen years old and just finishing up high school, I wrote down some personal goals. I had always been goal-oriented, and my mother encouraged me to write down my goals. One of those goals was to become the CEO of a major company. Even though I wrote it down, I knew it was as far off of a goal as I could have set. I didn't think there was any chance in the world of actually ever reaching that goal; in fact, I might as well have written that I was going to sprout wings and flap my way to the moon. And yet that became a powerful goal. It was my beacon in the fog.

I was very fortunate to have been able to get a good education. After graduating, I worked hard and had some incredible opportunities. I ended up having the opportunity to work as a CEO and a general manager at some large and well-known companies. Midway through my career in corporate America, I was given a leadership role in a large, international organization. I was eager and determined to earn my stripes, and I basically committed to do so at all costs. I was a very young general manager of the U.S. division, and I was determined to do anything that was necessary to succeed. My commitment bordered on insane. I had a young family, but I was traveling hundreds of thousands of miles every year. There were nights I would stay at the office all night long to do what I felt needed to be done. I was going to succeed, and I didn't care about the costs.

Then I learned the lesson that it is not worth risking everything of importance in your life to achieve success. The division I headed became very successful. In the middle of our run, my mentor and boss, Dr. Peter Horne, called my secretary and said, "I need to have a visit with Rich." That meant jumping on a plane, flying to Atlanta, then from Atlanta to Amsterdam, and from Amsterdam across the channel to Birmingham, England. Door-to-door, this was a twenty-two and a half hour trip.

When I arrived, Dr. Horne sat me down in his office. In his posh British accent, he said, "Rich, we're really delighted with the progress you've made in the USA market. Things are coming along rather nicely." And then he made this comment, which has stuck with me: "I want you to remember one thing, Rich. You can replace almost anything in this world. You can replace a car. You can replace a job. You can replace money. But you can't replace your health, you can't replace your trust relationships, and, most important, you can't replace your family." Then turning his hand upside down, he shooed me out of his office, and I began the long journey home.

Those twenty-two and a half hours, which I spent alone on a very crowded airplane, gave me plenty of time to think about what Dr. Horne had said. Most of my thoughts centered on my wife and children. For years I had been telling my wife, "This next project is a big one for me. I am going to give it my all for six months, so don't plan on seeing much of me. But once I finish it, things will be different." The six months would pass. I would complete the project, and then a new project would come along and I would start the cycle all over again. Those six months had turned into years as I kept promising, "If I give my all to this for six months, then we will have it made."

As I flew back across the Atlantic, I reflected on a trip I had taken to India some months before. When I got home, all of my sons and I came down with whooping cough, or pertussis. We had all been immunized, but somehow, we contracted this miserable illness. It was terrible. I remember coughing so hard that I would frequently vomit, but I lacked the discipline to take time off from my work to get better and help my wife with our sons. My youngest son at the time was Nathan. He was less than a year old when we all got sick, and it was life-threatening for him. In fact, he ended up in the hospital, where my wife took care of him because I was too busy.

Flying home, I realized I was falling into the "all or nothing trap," and I resolved that I was going to do better as a father and husband. The first thing I did when I got home was to gather my young sons together, give them each a hug, and tell them I love them. But when I went to pick up Nathan, he hollered and screamed. As he pushed me away, I realized he did not even know who I was. At that moment, I realized that achieving my goal of being a CEO was not worth losing the love of my family. And I began to change both my priorities and how I actually lived my life.

That doesn't mean I lost my intensity then or now. It doesn't mean that I never end up out of balance. But my short session with Dr. Horne brought great clarity to the fact that it's not worth giving up the things that matter most for the things that matter least. This insight was part of what helped me see the Zigzag Principle as a far better way to approach life.

Fast forward more than twenty years, Nathan is now grown, a successful businessman, and the revision 2.0 of me. He is a father of three children and an amazing father. He loves me, he supports me, and I can count on him. Standing six feet one inch tall and solid as a freight train, he unapologetically hugs me deeply every time he sees me. Let me ask you, did I make the right decision? What really matters? I know that for me, my sons, my wife, and the fully expressed love of my grandchildren are worth more than four jets, three Ferraris, and a vault full of gold.

Health now takes on a much deeper meaning for me than just food, water, and my body not being sick. Paying attention to my emotional health, my energy levels, my sense of knowing or spiritual health, and my mental health are equally, if not more, important than my physical health.

But my short session with Dr. Horne brought great clarity to the fact that it's not worth giving up the things that matter most for the things that matter least. This insight was part of what helped me see the Zigzag Principle as a far better way to approach life. Now, as I zig and zag from goal to goal, I still put intense effort into achieving my dreams. But at each turn, I've established a reward that for me inevitably includes my family (your rewards, of course, may differ). And for each goal I pursue, I set up guardrails that will determine the amount of time and effort I am willing to invest. There are not many ways to succeed without going out of balance for a period of time. The key is to realize that you are going out of balance for a short period and then bounce back and take some time off to enjoy your life.

I have another zigzag balance philosophy that differs dramatically from conventional wisdom. My philosophy involves a line of balance. Many people think you achieve balance by walking on the line of balance, by being at work exactly at 8 a.m. and leaving within minutes of 5 p.m., by getting eight hours of sleep each night, and by controlling life with a rigid schedule. I don't live my life that way. At times, I live my life extremely out of balance. I'll work so crazy hard that I think I'm going to die, and then I'll cross over and go for a cruise where I sleep eighteen hours a day. Then I'll charge back across the line and spend some incredible family time. Then I'll go work my guts out again and not sleep for a couple or three weeks while I start another new business. Then I'll spend a month in the Himalayas with my family. The way I define balance is not to try walking the perfect line but to cross that line of balance as frequently as possible. This is the final form of zigzagging I would suggest.

## THE LEGADO FAMILY FRAMEWORK

At this point in this closing chapter, I would like to introduce another stabilizing framework that has proven invaluable to many entrepreneurs throughout the world. This has been my thought leadership basis for the past several years, and it is called the Legado Family Framework.

The Legado Family Framework has been the core of my focus for the past four years. The fabric of our society is disintegrating, and the root cause is the deep human need for connection and community. Our families serve as the primary source of that profound stability and connection. As I approach the final chapters of my career, my focus has shifted from building and stabilizing businesses to securing our most crucial and rewarding assets: our families and the relationship we have with ourselves.

The Legado Family Framework is the very structure we implemented over twenty-five years ago to stabilize our family. It employs the foundational components of any enduring organization. It begins with a foundation of values and addresses the ancestral or epigenetic challenges that may have influenced us during our upbringing. On this foundation, we build pillars of Symbols, Traditions, Doctrine, and the often-overlooked Rites of Passage. Through these pillars, we can use our wealth—be it time, talents, or resources—to stabilize our families.

The base of the model is our core values. Most individuals, let alone families, have never even thought about, let alone defined, what those are. Without them, you simply cannot platform to stability. Equal to what values we seek, what destructive values do you desire to throw away? Most of us come with some significant negative epigenetic programming that we have to actually decide NOT to carry forward and throw in the garbage can.

On top of our core values are four vital pillars, I mentioned two paragraphs ago, that are required to sustain any social structure. They are symbols, doctrine, traditions, and rites of passage. Symbols identify us as part of the group; they are things like logos, colors, mascots, spirit animals. They unify us. Doctrine is things like mission statements, mantras, slogans, and songs. This guides our conduct in our tribe or family. In the absence of clear doctrine, rules are required. The more rules, the worse the definition of how we are expected to behave, which is the doctrine. The traditions are what bring us back to our family or tribe and make us feel safe—family dinners, bedtime stories for small children, or specific events at Thanksgiving dinner. This makes us feel part and unified. The final component is rites of passage. This is a lost art, and I go deeply into this in the Legado Family Framework. But what do you do to help your children, grandchildren, and great-grandchildren come of age and permanently embrace the core values? Our ancestors and indigenous tribes are great at this, but we have largely lost this beautiful art form.

Once we have this, we are prepared to stabilize our family with wealth. The meaning of wealth is not money; it is being well—emotionally, physically, spiritually, and financially well.

If this has piqued your interest, you can learn more about the Legado Family Framework at www.LegadoFamily.com. Below, I have included a working model of the Legado Family Framework.

## Legado Family Framework
by LEGADO

| 01 Symbols | 02 Traditions | 03 Doctrine | 04 Defining Events | 05 Structure |
|---|---|---|---|---|
| Color | Past & Present traditions | Mission Statement | Open Communication | Family Constitution |
| Mascot | Comings and goings | Slogan | Non- entitlement | Family Office |
| Logo | Meals | Mantra | Courage | Family Legacy |
| Word cloud | Routine | Beliefs | Capable | Family Bank |
| Apparel | Holidays | Yearly Theme | Independence | The Way2Wealth |
| Crest | Celebrate rights of passage | Goals | Contributions | |
| Spirit Animal | Daily Goodness | Big Rocks & Little Rocks | | |
| Food Sample | Annual Renewals | Touchstones | Age 8 | |
| | Calming Exercise | Song /Anthem/ Ballad | Age 12 | |
| | Set Up Routine | | Age 14 | |
| | Prayer for Thanksgiving | | Age 16 | |
| | | | Age 18 | |
| | | | Early Adulthood | |

**FOUNDATIONAL FAMILY VALUES**

# CYCLE OF FORCE AND CYCLE OF FLOW

None of the work that I talk about in the book or the work I do in Legado Family could be done without understanding the cycle of force and the cycle of flow. I am deeply grateful to my dear friend and collaborator, Scott Ford, for his contributions in developing the Infinite Entrepreneurship model that encompasses and explains these two cycles.

For many of us, life unfolds in a relentless cycle of force. We unwittingly perpetuate this cycle from one generation to the next, passing on the same destructive patterns that were once imposed upon us. The cycle comprises four core components: the individual internal relationship with yourself; intimate relationships within the family; our public persona and how we present ourselves to the world; and how we allocate our time, talents, and resources.

In the cycle of force, we must individually emerge from the grip of addictions, abuse, trauma, and a lack of self-awareness until we attain a balanced state that allows us to engage in healthy relationships. After a period of fostering healthy relationships, a desire for impact, starting a business, achieving fame, or some other public pursuit typically arises. This public phase often yields fireworks, self-aggrandizement, and what society might label as success.

Subsequently, we enter the final loop focused on wealth, encompassing not only monetary wealth but also how we invest our time, energy, and resources. When we neglect our core values in this phase, apathy creeps in, and value production diminishes, eventually leading to entitlement and a descent into the cycle's nadir. We must then begin the process anew.

The expressions "from rags to riches in three generations" and "the sins of the fathers rest on the children for seven generations" allude to these dynamics. Did you know that 70 percent of all financial resources held by wealthy families are lost by the second generation, and a staggering 90 percent are dissipated by the third?

How can we break free from this destructive cycle of force, not just for ourselves, but also for our children and grandchildren? The answer lies at the apex of the infinite loop, as depicted in the diagram (below). Achieving clarity regarding our individual values and ensuring they harmonize with our family values—which, in turn, align with our public-facing values, and coincide with our wealth values (how we invest our time, energy, and money)—mark the initial step in toppling the cycle of force and transitioning into a state of flow. I refer to this as "lubricating the system."

Yet, values alone are insufficient to disrupt the cycle of force. We must also eliminate the accumulated rust, grit, and grime from our lives to effect this change. This involves eradicating incongruencies, addressing epigenetic factors that have kept us stuck, and consciously choosing not to perpetuate the cycles of destruction that have been passed down through generations.

It is only when our personal, family, public-facing, and wealth values align that we can genuinely live in flow and experience joy.

Below are the visual diagrams that I use to indicate and walk through the Flow vs. Force Model.

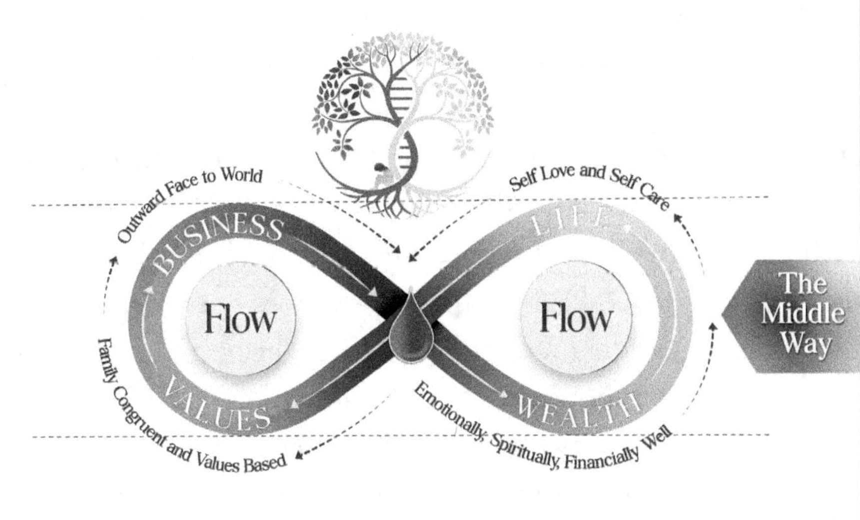
Living Life in a
Cycle of Flow
Outward Face to World
Self Love and Self Care
BUSINESS
LIFE
Flow
Flow
WEALTH
VALUES
The Middle Way
Family Congruent and Values Based
Emotionally, Spiritually, Financially Well

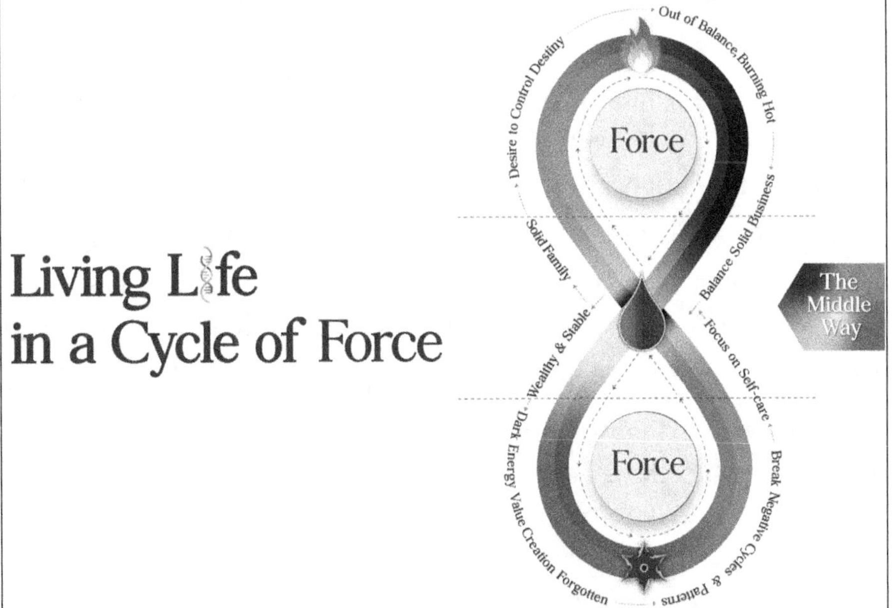
Living Life
in a Cycle of Force
Desire to Control Destiny
Out of Balance, Burning Hot
Force
Solid Family
Balance Solid Business
The Middle Way
Wealthy & Stable
Focus on Self-care
Dark Energy Value Creation Forgotten
Break Negative Cycles & Patterns
Force

This model ties in very closely with the Legado Family structure and has been a game changer not only for me, but for many with whom I work.

In the end, the Zigzag Principle will help us avoid the "all or nothing trap" as we work our way toward our beacons in the fog, whereas a straight line will lead us straight into the weeds.

I once listened to Jeff Sandefer, a university professor and Harvard MBA who *Bloomberg Businessweek* named one of the top entrepreneurship professors in the United States. Jeff spoke of a final exam he gave his MBA students, who were required to speak with ten seasoned and successful executives. Jeff further specified that the first three executives they interviewed needed to be highly successful, but under the age of thirty-five. The next three successful executives were to be in their mid-forties and fifties. The final four interviews were to be with successful executives who were in the final stages of their careers. In each of the interviews, Jeff's students were to elicit information on how these executives pursued and viewed success.

Invariably, the young bucks were beating their chests and chasing after the brass ring, often in ways that put them at risk of losing their balance. The middle-aged executives were beginning to figure life out. Some of them had regrets and others had chosen to add some balance to their lives.

Of course, it was the older executives who gave the real insight. It did not matter what type of business these men or women were involved with. In each case, they described a pattern of pursuing success that was guided by these three questions:

1. Was it honorable?

2.  Did it leave an impact?

3.  Who loves me and who do I love?

Many of these older executives were billionaires. And yet they talked very little about money. What mattered to them was how their business helped others and whether their business mattered. They wanted to leave a legacy. And most important, they talked about the people who loved them and the people they loved. Of course, there were those who did not have loved ones, and they talked about that absence with regret. They were honest and open and direct about their successes and their mistakes.

Whatever our goals are, whatever our beacon in the fog is, it is critical that we do what we do for the proper reasons and that we stay within the guardrails and values that we have set for ourselves. If we do, we will get to the end of our lives—a day which will inevitably come—and have no regrets.

## SUMMARY

In this chapter, you've learned the vital importance of avoiding the "all or nothing trap." Balancing your entrepreneurial ambitions with the foundational elements of life—family, trust relationships, and internal peace—is where true happiness lies.

Reflect on my journey and the wisdom shared by my mentor, Dr. Peter Horne. His advice about the irreplaceable nature of health, trust, and family reshaped my priorities. This insight was pivotal in developing the Zigzag Principle, guiding me to a more sustainable and fulfilling path.

Living in balance isn't about rigid schedules but about crossing the line of balance frequently, ensuring neither your professional nor personal life suffers. This balance allows you to work intensely yet take restorative time for yourself and with your family.

The Legado Family Framework, which I introduced, is a stabilizing model that has helped many entrepreneurs. It emphasizes core values, symbols, traditions, doctrine, and rites of passage to build strong, resilient families. This framework complements the Zigzag Principle, helping you navigate life's complexities while maintaining what matters most.

Understanding the cycle of force and the cycle of flow is crucial for achieving lasting success and joy. By aligning your values across personal, family, public, and wealth domains, you can break free from destructive cycles and live in harmony.

As you apply the Zigzag Principle, remember that avoiding the "all or nothing trap" leads to professional success and a life rich in meaningful relationships and personal well-being. This balanced approach ensures that when you reach the end of your journey, you are in flow and living a rich and full life free of regrets.

CHAPTER 10

# CONCLUSION

As we wrap up this journey together, let's revisit the key principles that underpin *The Zig Zag Principle*, a disciplined approach to business and life that requires immense effort but promises stability and strength.

## FOUNDATION:

➤ **Assess Resources:** Start by evaluating what you have at your disposal.

➤ **Set Your Beacon:** Determine your ultimate goal.

➤ **Adhere to Values:** Identify and uphold the values that guide your pursuit.

➤ **Fuel with Passion:** Drive your efforts with passion and determination.

# THE ZIGZAG APPROACH:

➤ **First Zig - Profitability:** Achieve profitability first. If not, pivot and try different strategies until success is achieved.

➤ **Second Zag - Resource Addition:** Use profits to add resources and involve others in your journey.

➤ **Third Zig - Scaling:** Work on your business, not just in it, to scale and grow.

# PLANNING AHEAD:

➤ **Three Zigs Ahead:** Always plan three zigs ahead, adjusting as necessary.

➤ **Guardrails:** Keep your zigs and zags within the bounds of your values and limitations.

➤ **Predetermined Resources:** Limit each step by the resources you can afford to commit.

➤ **Financial Targets:** Each zig should have a clear financial goal before moving to the next.

# REWARDS:

➤ **Motivation through Rewards:** Plan rewards to motivate you and your team at each milestone.

# AVOIDING THE ALL OR NOTHING TRAP:

➤ **Don't Risk What You Can't Afford to Lose:** Always avoid risking what you aren't willing to lose. Remember, you can replace many things, but you can't replace your family, your trusted relationships, and your health.

Reflecting on my journey from climbing mountains and exploring this majestic world, I realized that zigzagging, although counterintuitive, is the natural and effective way to reach our goals. While initially, I sought straight paths, my experiences in skiing, mountain climbing, and life taught me that zigzagging provides balance and control, allowing for greater success and sanity.

The Zigzag Principle extends beyond business, offering a flexible approach to any life goal, shifting the paradigm from "one strike and you're out" to a dynamic method of navigation. Missing the mark is acceptable, as long as you realign and continue toward your beacon.

There is profound satisfaction in reflecting on the paths we've taken, whether standing at the base of a ski slope with a son or atop a mountain with family. I hope you, too, will find joy in tracing your zigs and zags and reaching your summits.

Thank you for joining me on this journey through *The Zig Zag Principle.* I look forward to connecting with you and supporting your continued growth and success.

## A PERSONAL INVITATION

Over the past twelve years, my perspective has deepened, and I've developed more bridging content to help navigate the complexities of business and life. I invite you to reach out to me and utilize the resources available on my website www.RichChristiansen.com. Whether you need support in implementing these principles or navigating new challenges, I can connect you with experts who excel in these concepts.

I personally mentor three clients at a time, adhering to a non-negotiable set of guardrails for application to these slots. If you are interested, please let me know. At the end of the book I have included the best way to get in touch with me.

## INTRODUCING *BlindSighted*

I am thrilled to introduce my most recent book, *BlindSighted,* set to release in October 2024. This is my magnum opus, delving into the backstory that fueled my drive for success in business. *BlindSighted* is a journey of identity, faith, and healing, inspired by my own life experiences, including the revelation that I am one of the first donor-conceived children. My hope is that this book inspires you to confront your challenges and embark on a path of self-discovery and healing.

Many of you might be surprised that I've written such an intimate and personal book. How does this relate to *The Zig Zag Principle, Legado Family*, and my other books? In fact, it completes the narrative. Just like *The Lord of the Rings* became more powerful with the addition of *The Hobbit*, this book provides my personal story, background, and history, adding depth and context to *The Zig Zag Principle, Legado Family*, and my other works. It also completes what I call the cycle of flow.

To truly operate in flow, our values must align, and we need all aspects of our lives in harmony—our personal lives, family lives, intimate relationships, public-facing lives, and our wealth, including how we spend our time, money, and resources. *BlindSighted* shares my personal journey of achieving this flow and encourages you to face the demons and dragons in your own life.

# CONNECTING WITH RICH

You can connect with me, find the free value tools, and keep up to date with my latest content here:

Facebook
**https://www.facebook.com/richristiansen**

Instagram
**https://www.instagram.com/richristiansen_**

X
**https://x.com/richristiansen_**

LinkedIn
**https://www.linkedin.com/in/richristiansen**

Youtube
**https://www.youtube.com/@richristiansen**

TikTok
**https://www.tiktok.com/@richristiansen**

email:
**Rich@RichChristiansen.com**

Rich Christiansen is a globally-recognized thought leader, educator, mentor, parallel entrepreneur, and humanitarian. He has founded or co-founded 51 businesses and authored the best-selling *The Zig Zag Principle* and two other books, before releasing *BlindSighted*, his most personal book to date. When Rich isn't writing or helping others, he spends time throwing Frisbees with his sons and spelunking around the world with his wife.